One Knife,
One Pot,
One Dish

For my little chicks who are now roosters
and my shepherdess who raised them magnificently.

For my friends,
mates,
comrades,
partners in crime,
buddies . . .

and all those who have shared my table.

Acknowledgments

Thanks to the great Marabout and its team,

Ciniiiiiniiii, Rose, Audrey, and all the rest.

Thanks to Marie-Pierre,
hey now, the footy franks
have lost one of their friends,
where'd it go?

Happy birthday, Jacquy.

Stéphane Reynaud

One Knife, One Pot, One Dish

SIMPLE FRENCH FEASTS AT HOME

Abrams, New York

"Oh, cooking . . . it's too complicated!,"
some say, but it's not so:
Twenty minutes in the kitchen, at most;
simple ingredients; a knife; a pot;
a simmering dish that can be left in the oven,
taking its time, before coming to sit
in the middle of the table to the delight of all around it.

We disarm with a casserole,
turn heads with a baking dish,
nibble over drinks,
satisfy the vegan,
treat the vegetarian,
surprise the carnivore,
indulge with cheese,
smile at desserts . . . .

This book serves up a magic constellation
of fabulous food and fabulous meals.

Before
Dinner
9

Meat
19

Fish and
More
171

Eggs
209

Dips for Chips

Serves 6

For each dip, in a food processor, blend together all the ingredients, reserving a few items to use as garnishes. Serve with tortilla chips.

Food processor

Preparation time: 5 minutes each

Goat Cheese
7 ounces (200 g) fresh goat cheese
⅓ cup (50 g) unsalted nuts (hazelnuts, pistachios, walnuts . . .)
3 tablespoons olive oil
12 fresh Thai basil leaves

Corn
7 ounces (200 g) canned corn kernels, drained
3 tablespoons canola oil
1 shallot, peeled
6 pickled red chiles
Salt and black pepper

Guacamole
2 ripe avocados, pitted and peeled
Juice of 1 lemon
1 shallot, peeled
Dash of Tabasco sauce
⅓ cup (50 g) cherry tomatoes
Salt and black pepper

Hummus
About 1 cup (200 g) canned chickpeas, drained and rinsed
1 teaspoon ground cumin
1 clove garlic
6 tablespoons (100 ml) olive oil
3 sprigs fresh parsley
Salt and black pepper

Crostini Spreads

Serves 6

For each spread, in a food processor, blend together all the ingredients, reserving a few items to use as garnishes. Serve with toasted bread.

 Food processor

🕐 Preparation time: 5 minutes each

Anchovy
⅔ cup (100 g) anchovies in oil, drained
1 clove garlic
1 teaspoon pastis or other
    anise-flavored liqueur
Juice of 1 lemon
3 sprigs fresh tarragon

Black Olive
1 cup (150 g) pitted dry-cured black olives
8 fresh basil leaves
3 drained anchovies in oil, drained

Green Olive
1 cup (150 g) pitted green olives
1 clove garlic
½ cup (20 g) chopped fresh curly parsley
3 tablespoons olive oil

Sun-Dried Tomato
1⅓ cups (150 g) sun-dried
    tomatoes in oil, drained
⅓ cup (30 g) grated Parmesan cheese
1 teaspoon ketchup
2 tablespoons olive oil

Dips for Crudité

Serves 6

For each dip, in a food processor, blend together all the ingredients, reserving a few items to use as garnishes. Serve with sliced fresh vegetables.

Food processor

Preparation time: 5 minutes each

Tuna
8¾ ounces (250 g) tuna, drained
1 raw egg
1 teaspoon Dijon mustard
½ red onion, coarsely chopped
6 fresh chives, coarsely chopped
¼ cup (60 ml) olive oil
Salt and black pepper

Salmon and Cucumber
5¼ ounces (150 g) smoked salmon
3½ ounces (100 g) sliced cucumber, unpeeled
3 tablespoons (50 g) cream cheese
1 teaspoon fennel seeds

Sardine
5¼ ounces (150 g) boneless, skinless
    canned sardines, drained
4 fresh chives
1½ ounces (40 g) cornichons
½ shallot
4 fresh basil leaves
3 tablespoons olive oil
Salt and black pepper

Shrimp
5¼ ounces (150 g) peeled cooked shrimp
1 raw egg
1 teaspoon Dijon mustard
1 teaspoon ketchup
1 teaspoon cognac
¼ cup (60 ml) sunflower oil
Salt and black pepper

Popcorn

Serves 4

Dutch oven   Preparation time: 5 minutes each   Cooking time: 5 minutes each

Olive and Parmesan

About ½ cup (80 g) pitted dry-cured black olives
3 tablespoons olive oil
5 tablespoons (50 g) popcorn kernels
½ cup (50 g) finely grated Parmesan cheese

Coarsely chop the olives.

Heat the olive oil in a Dutch oven. Add the popcorn, cover, and shake the pan on the heat until most of the kernels have popped. Remove from the heat when the popping slows to a few seconds between pops.

Immediately add the Parmesan and olives and mix well.

Herb and Bacon

3 ounces (80 g) bacon, cut into matchsticks
5 tablespoons (50 g) popcorn kernels
1 tablespoon herbes de Provence
Salt

In a Dutch oven, cook the bacon until the fat has rendered and the bacon is crispy. Add the popcorn, cover, and shake the pan on the heat until most of the kernels have popped. Remove from the heat when the popping slows to a few seconds between pops.

Immediately add the herbes de Provence. Season with salt and mix well.

Soy Sauce and Basil

8 fresh basil leaves
3 tablespoons sunflower oil
5 tablespoons (50 g) popcorn kernels
3½ tablespoons (50 g) butter, melted
2 tablespoons sweet soy sauce (kecap manis)
Salt

Coarsely chop the basil leaves.

Heat the sunflower oil in a Dutch oven. Add the popcorn, cover, and shake the pan on the heat until most of the kernels have popped. Remove from the heat when the popping slows to a few seconds between pops.

Immediately add the the butter, soy sauce, and basil. Season with salt and mix well.

Curry and Lemon

2 tablespoons olive oil
5 tablespoons (50 g) popcorn kernels
Zest of 1 lemon
3½ tablespoons (50 g) butter, melted
1 teaspoon curry powder
Salt

Heat the olive oil in a Dutch oven. Add the popcorn, cover, and shake the pan on the heat until most of the kernels have popped. Remove from the heat when the popping slows to a few seconds between pops.

Immediately add the lemon zest, butter, and curry powder. Season with salt and mix well.

Beef with Mushrooms and Syrah

Serves 4

4 medium carrots, peeled
2 cloves garlic
4 shallots
2 pounds (1 kg) beef cheeks or brisket
7 ounces (200 g) mushrooms
3 sprigs fresh flat-leaf parsley
5¼ ounces (150 g) thick-cut bacon,
   cut into lardons
3½ tablespoons (50 g) butter
2 tablespoons all-purpose flour
2 cups (500 ml) beef stock
2 cups (500 ml) Syrah red wine
Bouquet garni (see Note)
Salt and black pepper

Dutch oven

320°F (160°C) oven

Preparation time: 10 minutes

Cooking time: 3 hours 15 minutes

Preheat the oven to 320°F (160°C).

Cut the carrots in half lengthwise. Crush the garlic. Finely chop the shallots. Cut the beef into large pieces. Clean the mushrooms gently with a damp paper towel. Chop the parsley.

In a Dutch oven over medium heat, sauté the bacon, shallots, and garlic in the butter. Add the beef and cook until browned. Sprinkle with the flour and brown again. Stir in the stock and wine, add the bouquet garni, carrots, and mushrooms, and season with salt and pepper. Cover and braise in the oven for 3 hours.

Sprinkle with the parsley before serving.

Note: A bouquet garni is a small bundle of fresh herbs tied together with kitchen twine, and often includes parsley, thyme, and bay leaf. Remove and discard the bouquet garni before serving.

Beef with Sesame Seeds and Vegetables

Serves 4

2 pounds (1 kg) beef cheeks or brisket
4 onions
4 medium carrots
4 small zucchini
3 tablespoons sunflower oil
2 stalks lemongrass
4½ cups (1 L) beef stock
1 tablespoon honey
Salt and black pepper
2 tablespoons sesame seeds

Dutch oven

320°F (160°C) oven

Preparation time: 10 minutes

Cooking time: 3 hours 15 minutes

Preheat the oven to 320°F (160°C).

Cut the beef into large pieces. Cut the onions into wedges. Slice the carrots and zucchini into rounds.

In a Dutch oven, heat the sunflower oil over medium heat. Add the beef and brown well. Add the onions, carrots, and lemongrass. Pour in the stock and honey, season with salt and pepper, cover, and braise in the oven for 3 hours.

Remove the lemongrass stalks. Garnish with the sesame seeds and serve topped with rounds of raw zucchini.

Beef with Beets and Peppers

Serves 4

1¾ pounds (800 g) beef cheeks or brisket
1 green bell pepper
1 red bell pepper
1 yellow bell pepper
4 baby beets
⅔ ounce (20 g) fresh ginger
3 spring onions
Greens from 1 bunch baby beets
2 tablespoons olive oil
⅔ cup (150 ml) red port
2 cups (500 ml) beef stock
Bouquet garni (see Note, page 20)
Salt and black pepper

Dutch oven

Preparation time: 10 minutes

Cooking time: 3 hours 15 minutes

Cut the beef into large pieces. Cut the bell peppers into thick strips. Peel the beets and ginger. Coarsely chop the onions. Chop the beet greens.

In a Dutch oven, heat the olive oil over medium heat. Add the beef and onions and cook until the beef is browned. Add the port, stirring to scrape up the browned bits from the bottom of the pot, then add the stock, bouquet garni, and ginger. Season with salt and pepper, cover, and cook over low heat for 2 hours.

Add the beets and bell peppers and cook for another hour.

Garnish with the beet greens and serve.

Short Ribs with Root Vegetables

Serves 4

2 parsnips
2 golden turnips
1 kohlrabi
3 onions
4 cloves garlic
1 shallot
3 sprigs fresh flat-leaf parsley
6 tablespoons (¾ stick/80 g) butter
2½ pounds (1.2 kg) bone-in beef short ribs
1¼ cups (300 ml) red wine
2½ cups (600 ml) beef stock
Salt and black pepper

Dutch oven

Preparation time: 15 minutes

Cooking time: 3 hours

Peel the parsnips, turnips, and kohlrabi and cut them into wedges. Thinly slice the onions, garlic, and shallot. Chop the parsley.

In a Dutch oven, melt the butter over medium heat. Add the ribs, onions, and garlic and cook until the ribs are browned on both sides.

Add the wine and stock, season with salt and pepper, cover, and cook over low heat for 2 hours.

Add all the root vegetables and cook for another hour (add a little water, if it looks dry).

Serve sprinkled with the parsley and shallot.

One-Pot Carbonnade

Serves 4

1¼ pounds (600 g) sirloin
4 onions
3½ tablespoons (50 g) butter
7 ounces (200 g) thick-cut bacon,
    cut into large lardons
1 tablespoon Demerara sugar
4½ cups (1 L) stout beer
Salt and black pepper
3 (½-inch/12-mm) slices pain d'épice
    (see Note)
1 tablespoon Dijon mustard

Dutch oven

Preparation time: 15 minutes

Cooking time: 2 hours 35 minutes

Cut the meat into small (½-inch/1-cm) cubes. Coarsely chop the onions.

In a Dutch oven over medium heat, melt the butter. Add the beef, onions, and bacon and cook, stirring, for 5 minutes. Add the sugar and let it caramelize.

Pour in the beer and season with salt and pepper.

Cut the bread into cubes, mix them with the mustard, and scatter them over the top of the dish. Cover and cook over low heat for 2 hours 30 minutes, checking periodically to be sure the stew is not drying out (add a little water if it is), and then serve.

Note: Pain d'épice (French spice bread) is sold in many markets, but if you have trouble finding it, gingerbread is a good substitute.

Beef Stroganoff

Serves 4

1¼ pounds (600 g) sirloin
7 ounces (200 g) mushrooms
3 spring onions
3½ tablespoons (50 g) butter
1 teaspoon paprika
½ cup (100 ml) white wine
1 tablespoon tomato paste
1 tablespoon ketchup
Salt and black pepper
1 teaspoon Dijon mustard
¼ cup (50 g) heavy cream

Dutch oven

Preparation time: 10 minutes

Cooking time: 20 minutes

Cut the meat into thin strips. Slice the mushrooms and spring onions.

In a Dutch oven over medium heat, melt the butter. Add the meat, onions, and mushrooms and cook, stirring, for 5 minutes.

Stir in the paprika. Add the wine, then the tomato paste and ketchup. Season with salt and pepper and simmer for 15 minutes.

Add the mustard and heavy cream, stir, and serve immediately.

Oxtail with Onions and Carrots

Serves 4

3 onions
4 medium carrots
3 cloves garlic
2½ pounds (1 kg) oxtail, cut into
    pieces, trussed
2 tablespoons tomato paste
4½ cups (1 L) vegetable stock
Salt and black pepper

Dutch oven

Preparation time: 10 minutes

Cooking time: 3 hours

Cut the onions and carrots into large chunks. Smash the garlic but do not peel it.

Place the oxtail in a Dutch oven, add the onions, carrots, garlic, and tomato paste, and cover with the stock.

Cook over low heat for 3 hours. Season with salt and pepper. Remove the string before serving.

Like a Pot-au-Feu

Serves 4

2 onions
4 orange carrots, with tops
4 purple carrots, with tops
1 bunch red radishes
1 bunch kale
3½ tablespoons (50 g) butter
1¾ ounces (50 g) thick-cut bacon,
    cut into lardons
4 thick slices chuck or flat-iron steak
    (2½ pounds/1 kg)
2 cups (500 ml) beef stock
Salt and black pepper
Bouquet garni (see Note, page 20)
2 cloves garlic, unpeeled

Dutch oven

Preparation time: 10 minutes

Cooking time: 2 hours 15 minutes

Slice the onions. Trim the carrot tops to about ½ inch (12 mm). Trim the radishes. Remove the kale leaves from the stems and discard the stems.

In a Dutch oven over medium heat, melt the butter. Add the bacon, onions, and beef and cook until the beef is browned. Stir in the stock. Season with salt and pepper. Add the bouquet garni and garlic, and cook over low heat for 1 hour 30 minutes.

Add the kale leaves, carrots, and radishes and cook for 30 minutes more, and then serve.

Chili

Serves 4

1 red bell pepper
1 green bell pepper
3 onions
4 cloves garlic
6 tablespoons (¾ stick/80 g) butter
1¼ pounds (600 g) ground beef
1⅓ cups (250 g) canned red kidney beans,
    drained and rinsed
1 cup (250 ml) tomato puree
3 tablespoons ketchup
1 teaspoon Tabasco sauce
1 tablespoon Worcestershire sauce
Salt

Dutch oven

Preparation time: 10 minutes

Cooking time: 30 minutes

Finely dice the bell peppers. Slice the onions. Crush the garlic.

In a Dutch oven over medium heat, melt the butter. Add the ground beef and onions and cook, stirring, for 10 minutes, or until the beef is well browned.

Add the bell peppers, garlic, beans, tomato puree, ketchup, Tabasco, and Worcestershire, cover, and cook over low heat, stirring regularly, for 20 minutes.

Season with salt before serving.

Macho Nachos

Serves 4

2 red onions
3½ ounces (100 g) pickled green chiles
    (about ¼ cup)
14 ounces (400 g) ground beef
1⅔ cups (400 ml) tomato puree
1 (14½-ounce/439-g) can red kidney
    beans, drained and rinsed
1 teaspoon ground cumin
1 teaspoon ground ginger
1 teaspoon ground nutmeg
3 tablespoons ketchup
Salt and black pepper
1½ cups (150 g) grated Gruyère cheese
⅔ cup (150 ml) heavy cream
Tortilla chips, for serving

Baking dish

350°F (180°C) oven

Preparation time: 10 minutes

Cooking time: 20 minutes

Preheat the oven to 350°F (180°C).

Finely chop the onions and chiles. In a bowl, mix half the chiles with the ground beef, onions, tomato puree, beans, spices, and ketchup; season with salt and pepper.

Pour the mixture into a baking dish.

In a small bowl, mix the Gruyère with the cream and the remaining chiles. Evenly top the ground beef mixture with the Gruyère mixture. Bake for 20 minutes.

Serve with tortilla chips for scooping.

Beef with Mushrooms and Bulgur

Serves 4

1¼ pounds (600 g) sirloin
7 ounces (200 g) mushrooms
3 shallots
3 cloves garlic
2 spring onions
¼ cup (½ stick/60 g) butter
Scant 1½ cups (200 g) bulgur
1½ cups (500 ml) vegetable stock
Salt and black pepper
Leaves from 1 bunch fresh basil

Dutch oven

Preparation time: 10 minutes

Cooking time: 20 minutes

Thinly slice the steak. Slice the mushrooms. Thickly slice the shallots, garlic, and spring onions.

In a Dutch oven over medium heat, melt the butter. Add the beef, mushrooms, shallots, garlic, and spring onions and cook, stirring, for 5 minutes.

Add the bulgur, pour in the stock, and season with salt and pepper. Cook over low heat for 15 minutes.

Shred the basil leaves and add them just before serving.

Short Ribs with Chiles and Fingerling Potatoes

Serves 4

3 shallots
4 cloves garlic
3 fresh Thai bird chiles
1¼ pounds (600 g) fingerling potatoes
2 tablespoons olive oil
¼ cup (60 ml) ketchup
¼ cup (60 ml) sweet soy sauce (kecap manis)
1 teaspoon ground ginger
¾ cup (200 ml) dry white wine
Salt and black pepper
2½ pounds (1.2 kg) bone-in beef short ribs

Baking dish

250°F (120°C) oven

Preparation time: 15 minutes

Cooking time: 3 hours

Preheat the oven to 250°F (120°C).

Coarsely chop the shallots, garlic, and chiles. Halve or quarter the fingerlings, depending on their size.

In a medium bowl, combine the shallots, garlic, chiles, olive oil, ketchup, soy sauce, ginger, and wine. Mix well to make a marinade and season with salt and pepper.

Place the meat in a baking dish in a single layer, pour over the marinade, and bake for 2 hours, turning the meat regularly.

Add the potatoes to the ribs and cook for 1 hour more and then serve.

Short Ribs with Roasted Onions and Potatoes

Serves 4

4 organic red onions, unpeeled (see Note)
3 tablespoons ketchup
1 tablespoon maple syrup
3 tablespoons soy sauce
6 tablespoons (¾ stick/80 g) butter
2½ pounds (1.2 kg) bone-in beef short ribs
Black pepper
8 baby potatoes

Dutch oven

250°F (120°C) oven

Preparation time: 10 minutes

Cooking time: 5 hours 15 minutes

Preheat the oven to 250°F (120°C).

Halve the onions. In a small bowl, mix together the ketchup, maple syrup, and soy sauce.

In a Dutch oven over medium heat, melt the butter. Add the ribs and brown on all sides. Cover with the sauce and season with pepper.

Arrange the onions and potatoes around the ribs, cover, and bake for 5 hours, checking occasionally to be sure the ribs aren't drying out; add a little water, if necessary. Serve the ribs with the onions and potatoes.

Note: Onion skins are very nutritious, high in fiber and antioxidants. Left unpeeled, onions cook in their own steam and become very tender. However, make sure the onions are organic (produced without pesticides); otherwise, the skins should not be eaten.

Roast Beef Provençal

Serves 4

4 cocktail toasts, or 1 slice bread, toasted
Leaves from 1 bunch fresh basil
2 cloves garlic
1 shallot
Salt and black pepper
1 (2-pound/1-kg) London broil, trussed
6 tablespoons (¾ stick/80 g) butter,
   at room temperature
1¼ pounds (600 g) mixed cherry or
   grape tomatoes
Fine sea salt

Food processor
Dutch oven or flameproof roasting pan

390°F (200°C) oven

Preparation time: 10 minutes

Cooking time: 20 minutes
Resting time: 10 minutes

Preheat the oven to 390°F (200°C).

In a food processor, pulse the cocktail toasts into coarse crumbs. Transfer to a bowl. In the food processor (no need to clean the bowl), combine the basil, garlic, and shallot and pulse until coarsely chopped. Transfer to the bowl with the toast crumbs and stir until well combined. Season with salt and pepper.

Rub the beef with the butter. In a Dutch oven or flameproof roasting pan, brown the beef on all sides over high heat.

Arrange the tomatoes around the beef, scatter with the Provençal crumb mixture, and roast for 15 minutes.

Rest the beef in a warm place by the oven for 10 minutes. Remove the string and slice thinly against the grain. Season with sea salt before serving.

Côte de Boeuf

Serves 4

1 (2-pound/1-kg) beef rib steak
Black pepper
Leaves from 2 sprigs fresh thyme
Leaves from 1 sprig fresh rosemary
6 tablespoons (¾ stick/80 g) butter
1 tablespoon sunflower oil
Coarse salt

Skillet
Large baking dish

400°F (205°C) oven

Preparation time: 5 minutes

Cooking time: 20 minutes
Resting time: 10 minutes

Preheat the oven to 400°F (205°C).

Season the steak with pepper and sprinkle with the herbs.

In a skillet, melt the butter with the sunflower oil over high heat. Add the steak and sear for 2 minutes on each side.

Sprinkle coarse salt over a baking dish, place the steak on top, and roast for 15 minutes, flipping the steak after 7 minutes.

Let it rest for 10 minutes in a warm place by the oven before serving.

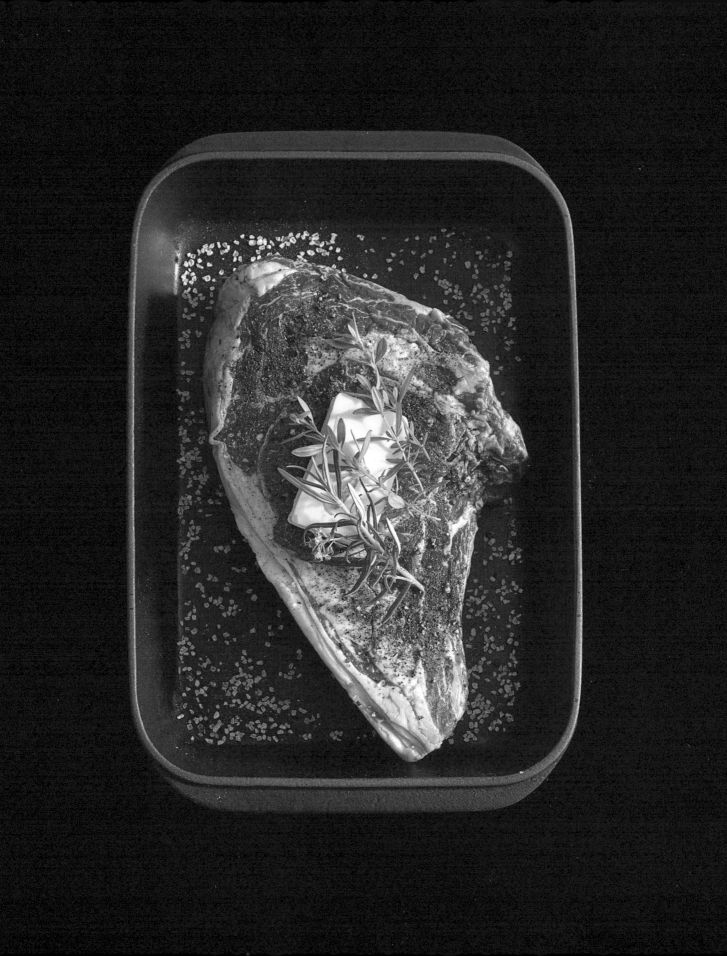

To Serve with Côte de Boeuf

Serves 4

 Skillet with lid
Saucepan

Preparation time: 10 minutes each

Cooking time: 5–20 minutes each

Easy Mash

1¼ pounds (600 g) Yukon Gold potatoes
¾ cup (200 ml) milk
½ cup (100 ml) heavy cream
6 tablespoons (¾ stick/80 g) butter
Salt and black pepper

Peel the potatoes and cut them into large cubes.

Combine the milk, cream, and butter in a saucepan.

Add the potatoes and cook over medium-low heat for 20 minutes, until they are soft. Mash them with a fork and season with salt and pepper, before serving.

Zucchini with Mint

3 zucchini
Leaves from 1 bunch fresh mint
3 tablespoons olive oil
Salt and black pepper

Quarter the zucchini lengthwise, remove the seeded cores, and slice. Chop the mint.

In a skillet, heat the olive oil over medium heat. Add the zucchini and cook for 5 minutes.

Remove from the heat, add the mint, and season with salt and pepper, before serving.

Chestnuts with Bacon and Onions

2 onions
3 slices thick-cut bacon, cut into lardons
14 ounces (400 g) vacuum-packed whole, cooked, peeled chestnuts
Salt and black pepper

Slice the onions.

In a skillet over medium heat, sauté the bacon with the onions for 5 minutes.

Add the chestnuts and cook for 10 minutes. Season with salt and pepper, before serving.

Onions with Herbs

4 organic red onions
6 tablespoons (¾ stick/80 g) butter
¾ cup (200 ml) white wine
Fine sea salt
2 tablespoons olive oil
Leaves from 1 bunch fresh herbs

Quarter the onions, leaving the skin on (see Note, page 44), and arrange them in a skillet.

Add the butter and wine, cover, and cook over medium heat for 15 minutes.

Season with salt, brush with olive oil, and serve sprinkled with the fresh herbs, before serving.

Easy Blanquette de Veau

Serves 4

3 onions
7 ounces (200 g) mushrooms
4 medium carrots
6 tablespoons (¾ stick/80 g) butter
2 pounds (1 kg) veal shoulder,
    cut into pieces
2½ cups (600 ml) veal stock
Salt and black pepper
7 ounces (200 g) shelled fresh peas
1 egg yolk
¾ cup (200 ml) heavy cream

Dutch oven
Skimmer

Preparation time: 15 minutes

Cooking time: 2 hours 5 minutes

Slice the onions. Quarter the mushrooms. Cut the carrots into pieces on an angle.

In a Dutch oven over medium heat, melt the butter. Add the veal and onions and cook until the veal is browned. Add the stock and bring to a boil, skimming off any foam that rises to the surface.

Add the carrots and mushrooms. Season with salt and pepper, cover, and cook over low heat for 1 hour 50 minutes. Add the peas and cook for 5 minutes more.

In a small bowl, mix the egg yolk with the cream. Add it to the blanquette, stir, and cook for 5 minutes, without letting the mixture boil (or the egg yolk will curdle), to warm through. Serve immediately.

Veal with Olives

Serves 4

4 shallots
2 cloves garlic
2 zucchini
1 medium carrot
3 sprigs fresh flat-leaf parsley
3 tablespoons olive oil
3½ ounces (100 g) thick-cut bacon,
    cut into lardons
1¼ pounds (600 g) veal shoulder,
    cut into pieces
1 tablespoon all-purpose flour
¾ cup (200 ml) white wine
1⅔ cups (400 ml) veal stock
2 tablespoons ketchup
2 bay leaves
Salt and black pepper
⅓ cup (50 g) pitted black olives
⅓ cup (50 g) pitted green olives

Dutch oven

Preparation time: 10 minutes

Cooking time: 2 hours

Slice the shallots. Crush the garlic. Medium dice the zucchini and carrot. Chop the parsley.

In a Dutch oven, heat the olive oil over medium heat. Add the shallots, garlic, and bacon and sweat them for 5 minutes. Add the veal and cook until browned on all sides, 5 minutes. Sprinkle with the flour and add the wine, stock, carrots, ketchup, and bay leaves. Season with salt and pepper. Simmer over low heat, stirring regularly, for 1 hour 45 minutes.

Add the olives and zucchini and cook for 5 minutes more. Sprinkle with parsley and serve immediately.

Spring Pot-au-Feu

Serves 4

1 pound (500 g) fresh peas in the pod
1 bunch asparagus
1 onion
2 whole cloves
1 bunch kale
4 baby leeks
1 large veal knuckle or shank (about
   2½ pounds/1 kg)
Bouquet garni (see Note, page 20)
6 cloves garlic, unpeeled
2 stalks celery, with their leaves
1 teaspoon whole black peppercorns
1 tablespoon coarse salt

Dutch oven
Skimmer

Preparation time: 10 minutes

Cooking time: 2 hours 15 minutes

Shell the peas. Halve the asparagus spears crosswise. Peel the whole onion and stud it with the cloves. Remove the kale leaves from stems and discard the stems. Trim the leeks.

Rinse the veal with cold water and place it in a Dutch oven. Pour in water to almost cover and bring it to a boil, skimming off any foam that rises to the top. Add the bouquet garni, onion, whole garlic cloves, whole celery stalks, peppercorns, and salt. Cook over low heat for 1 hour 30 minutes.

Remove and discard the bouquet garni, onion, garlic, and celery. Add the kale leaves and leeks and cook for 20 minutes more.

Add the peas and cook for 10 minutes more, before serving.

Osso Buco

Serves 4

3 onions
3 cloves garlic
4 ripe tomatoes
6 tablespoons (100 ml) olive oil
4 pieces cross-cut veal shanks (about
   2½ pounds/1 kg)
1 tablespoon all-purpose flour
1 tablespoon tomato paste
1¼ cups (300 ml) white wine
Salt and black pepper

Dutch oven

Preparation time: 10 minutes

Cooking time: 1 hour 45 minutes

Chop the onions and garlic. Cut the tomatoes into small wedges.

In a Dutch oven, heat the olive oil over medium heat. Add the pieces of veal, the onions, and the garlic and cook gently. Add the flour, let it brown, then add the tomatoes, tomato paste, and wine; season with salt and pepper.

Cook over low heat, stirring from time to time, for 1 hour 30 minutes, before serving.

Veal in Beet Broth

Serves 4

1¼ pounds (600 g) veal fillet
3 beets, with their tops
1 bunch multicolored radishes
4 baby carrots with their tops
3½ ounces (100 g) mushrooms
3½ tablespoons (50 g) butter
2 cups (500 ml) vegetable stock
3½ ounces (100 g) shelled fresh peas
10 fresh mint leaves
Salt and black pepper

Dutch oven

Preparation time: 15 minutes

Cooking time: 25 minutes

Thinly slice the veal fillet. Peel the beets, keeping their tops, and cut them in half lengthwise. Cut the radishes in half lengthwise, keeping their tops. Peel the carrots, keeping their tops. Clean the mushrooms and quarter them.

In a Dutch oven over medium heat, melt the butter. Add the veal and brown on all sides, then transfer it to a plate and set aside.

Add the stock to the pot and bring it to a boil. Add all the vegetables except the peas and cook over medium-low heat, uncovered, for 15 minutes. Add the veal, mint, and peas and cook for 5 minutes more.

Season with salt and pepper before serving.

Veal with Lemon and Mint

Serves 4

3 onions
6 ripe tomatoes
1 lemon
1 eggplant
Leaves from 1 bunch fresh mint
¼ cup (60 ml) olive oil
1¼ pounds (600 g) veal shoulder,
    cut into pieces
1⅔ cups (400 ml) vegetable stock
Salt and black pepper

Dutch oven

Preparation time: 15 minutes

Cooking time: 2 hours

Chop the onions. Medium dice the tomatoes, lemon, and eggplant discarding the seeds. Chop half the mint leaves.

In a Dutch oven, heat the olive oil over medium heat. Add the onions, eggplant, and veal and cook until the veal is lightly browned. Add the tomatoes, lemon, chopped mint, and stock; season with salt and pepper. Cook over low heat for 2 hours, checking periodically to make sure the pot hasn't dried out (add a little water if necessary).

Sprinkle with the rest of the mint leaves before serving.

Veal with Fennel and Celery Seed

Serves 4

2 onions
2 leeks
1 bone-in veal knuckle or shank (about
   2½ pounds/1 kg)
Bouquet garni (see Note, page 20)
2 fennel bulbs
1 teaspoon cracked black pepper
1 tablespoon coarse salt
3 tablespoons honey
3 tablespoons soy sauce
2 tablespoons celery seeds

Dutch oven
Baking dish (optional)

360°F (180°C) oven

Preparation time: 5 minutes

Cooking time: 2 hours 30 minutes

Quarter the onions and halve the leeks.

Put the veal in a Dutch oven. Add the bouquet garni, onions, leeks, whole fennel, pepper, and coarse salt. Add water to cover. Bring to a boil, then cook over low heat for 2 hours. Remove the veal and discard the vegetables. Clean and dry the Dutch oven.

Preheat the oven to 360°F (180°C).

In a small bowl, mix together the honey, soy sauce, and celery seeds.

Put the veal in the dry Dutch oven (or a baking dish) and cover with the honey sauce.

Bake for 30 minutes, basting the veal regularly with the sauce, and then serve.

Veal with Beets and Pomelo

Serves 4

2 sweet onions
3 beets
1 red onion
1 pomelo
1 (2-pound/1-kg) piece roasting veal,
   larded and trussed (see Note)
3 tablespoons olive oil
Salt and black pepper
¾ cup (200 ml) white wine

Baking dish

450°F (230°C) oven

Preparation time: 15 minutes

Cooking time: 45 minutes
Resting time: 15 minutes

Preheat the oven to 450°F (230°C).

Cut the sweet onions into wedges. Peel the beets and cut them into cubes. Slice the red onion into rings. Peel the pomelo and cut it into wedges.

Put the veal roast in a baking dish. Sprinkle with the olive oil, season with salt and pepper, and roast for 15 minutes.

Arrange the beets and sweet onions around the veal, pour in the wine, and bake for 30 minutes more.

Add the red onion and pomelo to the dish and let the roast stand in the oven with the door ajar for 15 minutes before serving.

Note: Larding and trussing is a way of preparing veal for roasting, where fat is inserted into the meat, which is then tied with string. You can ask your butcher to do this for you.

Veal with Turnips and Asparagus

Serves 4 on a cold night

1 bunch turnips
1 bunch green asparagus
1 head garlic
6 tablespoons (¾ stick/80 g) butter
2 tablespoons olive oil
1 (2½-pound/1.2-kg) rack of veal
¾ cup (200 ml) white wine
1¼ cups (300 ml) veal stock
12 fingerling potatoes
Salt and black pepper

Dutch oven

360°F (180°C) oven

Preparation time: 10 minutes

Cooking time: 50 minutes
Resting time: 10 minutes

Preheat the oven to 360°F (180°C).

Trim the turnip tops. Cut the asparagus and head of garlic in half crosswise.

In a Dutch oven, melt the butter with the olive oil over medium heat. Add the veal and brown the rack on all sides. Transfer the pot to the oven, uncovered, and bake for 20 minutes.

Add the wine, stock, turnips, asparagus, whole potatoes, and garlic. Season with salt and pepper, cover, and bake for 30 minutes more.

Turn off the oven and let the veal stand, uncovered, for 10 minutes before serving.

Hay-Baked Rack of Veal

Serves 4

4 red onions
6 tablespoons (¾ stick/80 g) butter
1 (2½-pound/1-kg) rack of milk-fed veal
¾ cup (200 ml) white wine
8 cloves garlic, unpeeled
Handful of clean, dry, culinary-grade hay
    (or alfalfa hay, see Note)
1 bunch fresh cilantro
Salt and black pepper

- Dutch oven
- 320°F (160°C) oven
- Preparation time: 10 minutes
- Cooking time: 1 hour 45 minutes

Preheat the oven to 320°F (160°C).

Quarter the onions.

In a Dutch oven, melt the butter over medium heat. Add the veal and brown the rack on all sides. Add the wine, onions, and garlic cloves.

Surround the veal with the hay and cilantro. Season with salt and pepper, cover, and bake for 1 hour 30 minutes. Discard the hay and serve.

Note: Roasting meat with hay lends a smoky, earthy flavor to the dish. Culinary hay is sold at specialty food markets or can be ordered online.

Cabbage with Bacon

Serves 4

4 onions
1 head cabbage
1 bunch fresh parsley
1 (1¼-pound/600-g) piece bacon
   or smoked pork belly
4½ cups (1 L) vegetable stock
¾ cup (200 ml) heavy cream
Black pepper

Dutch oven

Preparation time: 5 minutes

Cooking time: 1 hour 30 minutes

Slice the onions. Cut the cabbage into thin wedges. Chop the parsley.

Place the bacon in a Dutch oven and add the onions and cabbage. Pour in the stock, cover, and cook over medium-low heat for 1 hour 15 minutes.

Add the parsley and the cream, season with pepper, and cook, uncovered, for 15 minutes more, and then serve.

Pork with Dried Fruit and Mustard Seeds

Serves 4

3 shallots
2 pounds (1 kg) pork cheeks or shoulder
3½ tablespoons (50 g) butter
⅔ cup (100 g) dried apricots
⅔ cup (100 g) dried figs
¾ cup (100 g) pitted prunes
1 tablespoon mustard seeds
1¼ cups (300 ml) full-bodied red wine
1¼ cups (300 ml) vegetable stock
Salt and black pepper

Dutch oven

320°F (160°C) oven

Preparation time: 10 minutes

Cooking time: 1 hour 40 minutes

Preheat the oven to 320°F (160°C).

Halve the shallots lengthwise. If using pork shoulder, cut it into large pieces.

In a Dutch oven, melt the butter over medium heat. Add the pork and the shallots and cook until the pork is browned. Add the apricots, figs, prunes, mustard seeds, wine, and stock and season with salt and pepper.

Cover and bake for 1 hour 30 minutes, and then serve.

Pork with Coconut and Pineapple

Serves 4

1 ripe pineapple
4 shallots
2 ripe tomatoes
2 onions
1 mild chile
2 pounds (1 kg) pork cheeks or shoulder
1 tablespoon sunflower oil
1 tablespoon curry powder
1 teaspoon ground ginger
1⅔ cups (400 ml) coconut milk
Salt and black pepper
Juice of 1 lime
Leaves from 1 small bunch fresh cilantro

Dutch oven

Preparation time: 15 minutes

Cooking time: 1 hour 45 minutes

Peel the pineapple, remove the eyes, and cut it into small cubes. Finely chop the shallots. Chop the tomatoes. Quarter the onions. Cut the chile into thin strips. If using pork shoulder, cut it into large pieces.

In a Dutch oven, heat the sunflower oil over medium heat. Add the pork, curry, and ginger and cook, stirring, to brown the pork. Add the onions, shallots, tomatoes, chile, and pineapple. Pour in the coconut milk and season with salt and pepper.

Cover and cook over low heat, stirring occasionally, for 1 hour 30 minutes.

Just before serving, sprinkle with the lime juice and scatter the cilantro over the top.

Pork with Green Peppercorns and Shiitakes

Serves 4

2 red onions
14 ounces (400 g) shiitake mushrooms
4 cloves garlic
4 fresh chives
2 pounds (1 kg) pork cheeks or shoulder
3 tablespoons olive oil
6 tablespoons (100 ml) white port
1 tablespoon green peppercorns
2 cups (500 ml) vegetable stock
Salt

Dutch oven

320°F (160°C) oven

Preparation time: 5 minutes

Cooking time: 1 hour 45 minutes

Preheat the oven to 320°F (160°C).

Slice the onions and the mushrooms. Crush the garlic. Chop the chives. If using pork shoulder, cut it into large pieces.

In a Dutch oven, heat the olive oil over medium heat. Add the garlic and onions and cook, stirring, then add the pork and brown it. Add the port, scraping up any browned bits from the bottom of the pot, then add the mushrooms, peppercorns, and stock. Season with salt. Cover and bake for 1 hour 30 minutes.

Sprinkle with the chives at serving time.

Pork with Berries and Tomatoes

Serves 4

2 onions
1¾ ounces (50 g) fresh ginger
¼ cup (½ stick/50 g) butter
1¾ pounds (800 g) pork neck or shoulder
¾ cup (200 ml) white wine
9 ounces (250 g) frozen mix of red fruits
    and berries
3 tablespoons ketchup
¾ cup (200 ml) veal stock
Salt

Dutch oven

300°F (150°C) oven

Preparation time: 10 minutes

Cooking time: 2 hours 45 minutes

Preheat the oven to 300°F (150°C).

Slice the onions. Peel and chop the ginger.

In a Dutch oven, melt the butter over medium heat. Add the pork, onions, and ginger and brown the pork on all sides. Add the wine, cover, and bake for 1 hour 30 minutes.

Add the berries, ketchup, and stock. Season with salt and bake for 1 hour more, and then serve.

MEAT

Pork Pot-au-Feu

Serves 4

4 leeks
2 zucchini
2 onions
2 whole cloves
7 ounces (200 g) salt-cured pork spare ribs
4 slices thick-cut bacon (about 7 ounces/
   200 g per slice)
4 medium carrots
4½ cups (1 L) vegetable stock
4 slices sabodet (pig's-head-and-skin sausage)
   or pork sausage, if unavailable
4 slices cervelas de Lyon (pork sausage with
   pistachios, see Note)

Dutch oven

Preparation time: 15 minutes

Cooking time: 2 hours

Halve the leeks lengthwise, then crosswise. Quarter the zucchini lengthwise, then cut it crosswise into 2-inch (5-cm) long pieces. Peel the onions and stud each whole onion with one clove.

Put the spare ribs and bacon in a Dutch oven with the carrots, onions, leeks, and stock. Cover and cook over low heat for 1 hour 30 minutes.

Add the sabodet, cervelas sausage, and zucchini and cook for 30 minutes more, and then serve.

Note: If the sabodet and cervelas de Lyon are unavailable, feel free to replace these with two different kinds of your favorite sausages.

MEAT

Pork with Corn

Serves 4

2 medium carrots
1 onion
2 whole cloves
1 (2½-pound/1-kg) pork knuckle
4 ears of corn, husked
Bouquet garni (see Note, page 20)
1 tablespoon coarse salt

Dutch oven

Preparation time: 5 minutes

Cooking time: 3 hours

Slice the carrots into rounds. Peel the whole onion and stud it with the cloves.

Place the pork knuckle in a large Dutch oven and arrange the corn around it.

Add the bouquet garni, onion, and carrots. Add the salt and water to cover. Cover, bring to a boil, then reduce the heat to low and cook for 3 hours, before serving.

Pork with Pumpkin and Peanuts

Serves 4

1 Hokkaido pumpkin (red kuri squash)
3 shallots
4 ripe tomatoes
½ cup (80 g) roasted salted peanuts
2 pounds (1 kg) pork neck or shoulder, trussed
Salt and black pepper
1 tablespoon peanut oil
2 sprigs fresh thyme
1 sprig fresh rosemary
3½ tablespoons (50 g) butter
¾ cup (200 ml) vegetable stock

Dutch oven

320°F (160°C) oven

Preparation time: 15 minutes

Cooking time: 2 hours 15 minutes

Preheat the oven to 320°F (160°C).

Small dice the pumpkin, keeping the skin on. Remove the seeds. Finely chop the shallots. Cut the tomatoes into wedges. Coarsely chop the peanuts.

Season the pork with salt and pepper. In a Dutch oven, heat the peanut oil over medium heat. Add the pork, shallots, thyme, rosemary, and butter and brown the pork on all sides. Pour in the stock.

Cover and bake for 1 hour, turning the pork regularly and basting from time to time with the stock. Add the tomatoes and pumpkin, cover, and bake for 1 hour more.

Scatter the peanuts over the dish before serving.

Pork with Tomatoes and Black Trumpet Mushrooms

Serves 4

2 ounces (50 g) dried black trumpet
   mushrooms
6 ripe tomatoes
2 onions
1 bunch fresh cilantro
¼ cup (½ stick/60 g) butter
1¾ pounds (800 g) pork neck or shoulder,
   trussed
2 ounces (50 g) green peppercorns
1 stalk lemongrass
6 tablespoons (100 ml) white port
1¼ cups (300 ml) veal stock
Salt

Saucepan
Dutch oven

320°F (160°C) oven

Preparation time: 10 minutes

Cooking time: 2 hours 30 minutes

Preheat the oven to 320°F (160°C).

Bring a saucepan of water to a boil. Put the dried mushrooms in a bowl and pour over the boiling water to cover. Set aside to soak for 5 minutes, then drain, discarding the soaking liquid.

Cut the tomatoes into wedges. Slice the onions. Chop the cilantro.

In a Dutch oven, melt the butter over medium heat. Add the pork and onions and brown the pork on all sides. Add the mushrooms, tomatoes, cilantro, peppercorns, lemongrass, port, and stock. Season with salt.

Cover and bake for 2 hours 30 minutes, checking periodically to make sure the pot isn't drying out (add a little water, if necessary). Remove the lemongrass and string before serving.

Pork with Jerusalem Artichokes and Cilantro

Serves 4

5 cloves garlic
1¾ pounds (800 g) Jerusalem artichokes
4½ pounds (2 kg) coarse salt
2 pounds (1 kg) pork neck or shoulder
1 bunch fresh cilantro

Dutch oven

320°F (160°C) oven

Preparation time: 5 minutes

Cooking time: 2 hours
Resting time: 15 minutes

Preheat the oven to 320°F (160°C).

Thinly slice the garlic. Peel the Jerusalem artichokes.

Cover the bottom of a Dutch oven with some of the coarse salt. Put the pork and Jerusalem artichokes in the pot, top with the garlic and cilantro, then cover it all with the remaining salt.

Bake for 2 hours. Let the roast rest for 15 minutes before breaking the salt crust. Slice the pork and brush off any excess salt, if desired, before serving with the Jerusalem artichokes.

Pulled Pork

Serves 4

2 onions
1 tablespoon coriander seeds
1 tablespoon ground cumin
1 teaspoon cracked black pepper
2 tablespoons tomato paste
3 tablespoons olive oil
3 pounds (1.5 kg) pork neck or shoulder
Fine sea salt

Dutch oven

265°F (130°C) oven

Preparation time: 10 minutes

Cooking time: 5 hours

Preheat the oven to 265°F (130°C).

Coarsely chop the onions. In a small bowl, stir together the coriander seeds, cumin, pepper, tomato paste, and olive oil.

Put the pork in a Dutch oven and coat it with the spice mixture. Add the onions and season with salt. Cover and bake for 5 hours.

Shred the meat with a fork and serve.

Note: Leftovers of this dish can be used to make tacos (see page 102).

Spare Ribs with Honey and Arugula

Serves 4

¼ cup (60 ml) honey
¼ cup (60 ml) soy sauce
¾ cup (200 ml) chicken stock
4 yellow beets
4 baby turnips
1 onion
2 whole cloves
2 pounds (1 kg) pork spare ribs
Bouquet garni (see Note, page 20)
4 baby carrots
7 ounces (200 g) shelled fresh peas
1 handful arugula
Salt and black pepper
3 tablespoons olive oil

Dutch oven or flameproof baking dish

320°F (160°C) oven

Preparation time: 10 minutes

Cooking time: 1 hour 15 minutes

Preheat the oven to 320°F (160°C).

In a small bowl, mix together the honey, soy sauce, and stock.

Peel and halve the beets. Peel the turnips. Peel the whole onion and stud it with the cloves.

Bring a Dutch oven or flameproof baking dish full of salted water to a boil. Add the spare ribs, bouquet garni, and onion and simmer for 45 minutes. Add the beets, turnips, and carrots and cook for 15 minutes more.

Remove the ribs, setting them aside on a plate, and strain the stock, reserving the vegetables.

Return the ribs to the pan, moisten with some stock, and bake for 15 minutes. Coat the ribs with the honey mixture. Add the reserved vegetables and peas, season with salt and pepper, sprinkle with arugula, and dress with olive oil before serving.

MEAT

Spare Ribs with Vegetables

Serves 4

2 racks pork spare ribs, 8 ribs each
4 cloves garlic
1 lemon
7 tablespoons (100 g) butter
½ cucumber
½ bunch radishes
1 red onion
1 tablespoon harissa paste
1 teaspoon paprika
1 teaspoon dried thyme
14 ounces (400 g) canned corn kernels,
    drained
Fine sea salt

Large baking dish

280°F (140°C) oven

Preparation time: 15 minutes

Cooking time: 1 hour 30 minutes

Preheat the oven to 280°F (140°C).

Cut the pork racks into ribs.

Finely chop the garlic. Zest and juice the lemon. Cut the butter into pieces.
Cut the cucumber into quarter rounds and the radishes into wedges or
rounds. Slice the onion.

In a small bowl, mix the harissa, lemon zest and juice, garlic, paprika,
and thyme.

Brush the ribs with the harissa mixture and put them in a baking dish.
Dot with the butter. Bake for 1 hour 15 minutes. Add the corn and bake for
15 minutes more.

Season with salt. Scatter the cucumber, radish, and onion over the ribs
before serving.

MEAT

Roast Rack of Pork

Serves 4

1 tablespoon herbes de Provence
Juice of 1 lemon
3 tablespoons olive oil
1 (2½-pound/1.2-kg) rack of pork
Fine sea salt
¾ cup (200 ml) white wine
4 spring onions
8 cloves garlic

Baking dish

390°F (200°C) oven
then 300°F (150°C)

Preparation time: 5 minutes
Marinating time: 1 hour

Cooking time: 1 hour 30 minutes

In a small bowl, mix the herbes de Provence, lemon juice, and olive oil.

Put the rack of pork in a baking dish, brush it with the herb mixture, and season with salt. Marinate for 1 hour, uncovered.

Preheat the oven to 390°F (200°C).

Bake for 30 minutes, turning regularly, then reduce the oven temperature to 300°F (150°C). Pour over the wine, arrange the spring onions and garlic around the rack, and cook for 1 hour more.

Slice and then serve.

To Serve with the Rack of Pork

Serves 4

⊓ Skillet   ⏱ Preparation time: 10 minutes each   〰 Cooking time: 0–45 minutes each

Apricots with Hazelnuts and Rosemary

12 fresh ripe apricots
6 tablespoons (¾ stick/80 g) butter
1 sprig fresh rosemary
¾ cup (80 g) chopped hazelnuts
Fine sea salt

⊱ Halve and pit the apricots.

▭ Melt the butter in a skillet over medium heat and cook until it takes on a nutty color.

◎ Add the apricots, rosemary sprig, and hazelnuts and cook for 5 minutes. Season with salt, before serving.

Champignons à la Crème

14 ounces (400 g) mushrooms
2 onions
4 fresh chives
2 tablespoons olive oil
1¼ cups (300 ml) heavy cream
Salt and black pepper

⊱ Thinly slice the mushrooms. Chop the onions and the chives.

▭ In a skillet, heat the olive oil over medium heat. Add the mushrooms and onions and cook until the mushrooms release all their liquid.

◎ Add the cream and cook for 5 minutes. Season with salt and pepper and sprinkle with the chives, before serving.

Eggplant Bohémienne

2 eggplants
2 ripe tomatoes
2 onions
4 cloves garlic
6 tablespoons (100 ml) olive oil
Salt and black pepper

⊱ Cut the eggplants and tomatoes into ⅜-inch (1-cm) dice. Chop the onions. Crush the garlic.

▭ Heat the olive oil in a skillet over medium heat. Add the eggplant, onions, and garlic. Cook, stirring, for 15 minutes.

◎ Add the tomatoes and cook for 30 minutes. Season with salt and pepper, before serving.

Arugula and Orange Salad

1 orange
¼ cup (60 ml) olive oil
¼ red onion
2 handfuls arugula
Salt and black pepper

⊱ Zest the orange and mix the zest with the olive oil. Peel the orange with a knife. Stand it on the cutting board and cut around the orange to remove the pith. Cut between the membranes to release the segments. Slice the red onion into a few rings.

◎ In a medium bowl, mix the arugula with the olive oil mixture. Add the orange segments, season with salt and pepper, and scatter a few onion rings over the top, before serving.

Pork Tacos

Serves 4

1 red bell pepper
1 green bell pepper
1 yellow bell pepper
4 cloves garlic
2 onions
6 sprigs fresh parsley
2 Thai bird chiles
2 tablespoons olive oil
14 ounces (400 g) leftover pulled pork
    (page 92)
1¼ cups (300 ml) vegetable stock
2 tablespoons tomato paste
Salt
Fresh flour or corn tortillas, for serving

Dutch oven

Preparation time: 10 minutes

Cooking time: 25 minutes

Thinly slice the bell peppers. Coarsely chop the garlic and onions. Chop the parsley and chiles.

In a Dutch oven, heat the olive oil over medium heat. Add the pork, all the vegetables, the chiles, and the parsley and cook for 5 minutes. Pour in the stock, add the tomato paste, season with salt, and cook over low heat for 20 minutes more, until heated through.

Serve with tortillas and any other taco toppings as desired.

Pork with Apples and Soy Sauce

Serves 4

4 shallots
2 pounds (1 kg) pork belly
2 tablespoons white vinegar
Black pepper
4 Granny Smith or other tart apples
¾ cup (200 ml) sweet soy sauce
   (kecap manis)
¾ cup (200 ml) beef stock

Box cutter
Dutch oven or baking dish

360°F (180°C) oven
then 250°F (120°C)

Preparation time: 15 minutes

Cooking time: 3 hours

Preheat the oven to 360°F (180°C).

Finely chop the shallots. Score the skin of the pork belly in a crisscross pattern using a clean box cutter, rub with the vinegar, and season with pepper. Cut the apples into wedges and core them.

Put the pork in a Dutch oven or baking dish and bake for 30 minutes.

Add the shallots, soy sauce, and stock, reduce the oven temperature to 250°F (120°C), and bake for 2 hours 15 minutes more.

Add the apples and bake for 15 minutes more, and then serve.

Pork with Beer and Tomatoes

Serves 4

3 shallots
4 cloves garlic
6 ripe tomatoes
1 red bell pepper
1 large (2½-pound/1-kg) pork leg steak
¼ cup (60 ml) olive oil
Salt and black pepper
2 cups (500 ml) pale beer, plus more if needed

Baking dish

320°F (160°C) oven

Preparation time: 10 minutes

Cooking time: 2 hours

Preheat the oven to 320°F (160°C).

Quarter the shallots and garlic. Medium dice the tomatoes and bell pepper.

Brush the leg steak with the olive oil, season with salt and pepper, and put it in a baking dish. Surround it with the vegetables and bake for 20 minutes.

Pour in the beer and cook for 1 hour 40 minutes more, checking occasionally and adding a little more beer if the baking dish looks dry, before serving.

Sausages with Lentils and Cumin

Serves 4

3 shallots
3 tablespoons olive oil
1 cup (200 g) blue-green Puy lentils
1 tablespoon cumin seeds
2 cups (500 ml) chicken stock
Salt and black pepper
4 sausages from your corner of
    the world

Dutch oven or flameproof baking dish

360°F (180°C) oven

Preparation time: 5 minutes

Cooking time: 50 minutes.

Preheat the oven to 360°F (180°C).

Finely chop the shallots.

In a Dutch oven or flameproof baking dish, heat the olive oil over medium heat. Add the shallots and cook, stirring. Add the lentils, cumin, and stock and season with salt and pepper.

Arrange the sausages over the lentils, cover with a sheet of parchment paper pierced in the middle, and bake for 45 minutes, and then serve.

 MEAT

Sausages and Beans

Serves 4

3 spring onions
4 Toulouse sausages or kielbasa or
    any pork sausage
3 slices thick-cut bacon, cut into large
    lardons
A few fresh Thai basil leaves
Leaves from 3 sprigs fresh rosemary
3 tablespoons (50 ml) cognac
¾ cup (200 ml) vegetable stock
1⅓ cups (250 g) canned white beans,
    drained and rinsed
Salt and black pepper

Dutch oven

Preparation time: 5 minutes

Cooking time: 15 minutes

Slice the spring onions, including the stems. Cut the sausages in two crosswise, if desired. Cut the basil into ribbons.

In a Dutch oven over medium heat, sauté the sausages and the bacon for 10 minutes. Add the onions and rosemary leaves. Add the cognac and, using a long kitchen match or barbecue lighter, very carefully flambé. When the flames have cooked off, add the stock, stirring to scrape up any browned bits on the bottom of the pan, add the beans, and simmer for 5 minutes. Season with salt and pepper.

Serve garnished with the basil.

Hot Dogs with Cheese

Serves 4

3 onions
3 tablespoons ketchup
1 tablespoon Dijon mustard
2 tablespoons barbecue sauce
8 good-quality hot dogs
4 slices Emmental cheese

Baking dish

360°F (180°C) oven

Preparation time: 5 minutes

Cooking time: 15 minute

Preheat the oven to 360°F (180°C).

Slice the onions.

In a medium bowl, mix together the ketchup, mustard, and barbecue sauce and add the onions to this mixture.

Arrange the hot dogs in a baking dish, cover with the onion mixture, top evenly with the cheese, and bake for 15 minutes, until the cheese melts.

Serve immediately.

Rice with Pork Sausage and Lime

Serves 4

1 cervelas de Lyon (pork sausage with pistachios, or any pork sausage, if unavailable)
3 spring onions
1 heaping cup (200 g) basmati rice
6 tablespoons (100 ml) white wine
1¼ cups (300 ml) chicken stock
1 generous handful arugula
3 tablespoons olive oil
2 limes, cut into wedges
Salt

Dutch oven or flameproof baking dish
390°F (200°C) oven
Preparation time: 10 minutes
Cooking time: 20 minutes

Preheat the oven to 390°F (200°C).

Slice the sausage into rounds. Thinly slice the spring onions, including their stems.

In a Dutch oven or flameproof baking dish over medium heat, brown the sausages. Add the onions and rice. Pour in the wine and stock, cover with a sheet of parchment paper pierced in the middle, and bake for 15 to 20 minutes, until the rice is tender.

Dress the arugula with the olive oil, scatter it over the dish, and serve with the limes. Taste and season at the table; the sausage might be salty enough to season the dish.

Reblochon and Bacon Gratin

Serves 4

14 ounces (400 g) fingerling potatoes
3 onions
4 shallots
6 fresh chives
1 Reblochon cheese (about 1 pound/500 g)
7 ounces (200 g) thick-cut bacon,
    cut into lardons
¾ cup (200 ml) white wine
Cracked black pepper
Toasted baguette slices (optional)

Dutch oven

Preparation time: 10 minutes

Cooking time: 40 minutes

Halve the potatoes. Chop the onions, shallots, and chives. Thinly slice the cheese.

Put the potatoes in a Dutch oven, add water to cover, and bring it to a boil. Cook for 20 minutes, then drain. Dry the pot.

In the dry pot, sauté the bacon, onions, and shallots over medium heat. Add the potatoes, cheese, and chives. Add the wine and cook over low heat for 15 minutes, until the cheese has melted.

Season with pepper before serving with toasted bread, if desired.

Simple Lamb Shoulder

Serves 4

1¼ pounds (600 g) fingerling potatoes
2 organic unwaxed oranges
2 heads garlic
1 (2½-pound/1.2-kg) boneless lamb
    shoulder, rolled and trussed
3 tablespoons olive oil
Salt and cracked black pepper
4 mild chiles
1¼ cups (300 ml) vegetable stock

Large baking dish

360°F (180°C) oven

Preparation time: 10 minutes

Cooking time: 1 hour 15 minutes

Preheat the oven to 360°F (180°C).

Halve the potatoes and cut the orange into wedges, leaving the skin on. Slice the top third off the heads of garlic to expose the cloves.

Put the lamb in a baking dish and drizzle with the olive oil. Season with salt and pepper, add the garlic, and bake for 30 minutes.

Arrange the potatoes, orange wedges, and whole chiles around the lamb, pour in the stock, and bake for 45 minutes more.

Remove the string and slice before serving.

Lamb with Carrots and Sweet Onions

Serves 4

3 sweet organic onions, unpeeled
1 bunch baby carrots
¼ cup (60 ml) olive oil
1 (2½-pound/1.2-kg) boneless
    lamb shoulder
6 cloves garlic
1 sprig fresh rosemary
2 sprigs fresh thyme
¾ cup (200 ml) dry white wine
Salt and black pepper

Dutch oven

360°F (180°C) oven

Preparation time: 5 minutes

Cooking time: 55 minutes
Resting time: 10 minutes

Quarter the onions (keeping their skins on). Peel and trim the carrots.

Heat the olive oil in a Dutch oven over medium heat. Add the lamb shoulder and brown on all sides.

Add the onions, carrots, garlic, rosemary sprig, thyme sprigs, and wine and season with salt and pepper.

Cover and bake for 30 minutes. Remove the lid and bake for 15 minutes more.

Let it rest for 10 minutes before serving.

Lamb with Anchovies and Red Endives

Serves 4

4 cloves garlic
4 red endives
1 red onion
10 fresh chives
1 (2½-pound/1.2-kg) half lamb-leg roast
2 ounces (50 g) salted anchovy fillets
¼ cup (60 ml) olive oil
1¼ cups (300 ml) lamb or veal stock
Fine sea salt and black pepper

Roasting pan

475°F (245°C) oven
then 390°F (200°C)

Preparation time: 10 minutes

Cooking time: 35 minutes
Resting time: 10 minutes

Preheat the oven to 475°F (245°C).

Quarter each garlic clove. Halve the endives lengthwise. Slice the onion into rings. Snip the chives into ½-inch (1-cm) lengths.

Make small slits in the leg of lamb and insert a piece of garlic and an anchovy in each slit. Rub the lamb with the olive oil. Put the lamb in a roasting pan and roast for 10 minutes. Reduce the oven temperature to 390°F (200°C) and roast for 15 minutes more.

Arrange the endives around the lamb, pour in the stock, cover with a sheet of aluminum foil, and bake for 10 minutes more.

Let it rest for 10 minutes before serving, decorated with the onion and chives. Have your guests season their lamb with salt and pepper after tasting: The anchovies can be very salty.

Lamb with Potatoes and Herbs

Serves 4

2 cloves garlic
2 bunches fresh basil
3½ tablespoons (50 g) butter, at room
   temperature
Fine sea salt
4 Yukon Gold potatoes
1 (2½-pound/1.2-kg) leg of lamb
6 tablespoons (100 ml) olive oil, plus more
   as needed

Roasting pan

360°F (180°C) oven

Preparation time: 10 minutes

Cooking time: 1 hour 40 minutes
Resting time: 10 minutes

Preheat the oven to 360°F (180°C).

Finely chop the garlic and 8 of the basil leaves. In a small bowl, combine the chopped garlic and basil with the butter and mash together using a fork. Season with salt.

Halve each potato, place a quarter of the herb butter on one half and sandwich it closed, then wrap the potatoes individually in aluminum foil.

Put the lamb in a roasting pan. Rub the lamb with most of the olive oil and sprinkle with salt. Toss the remaining basil with a bit of olive oil and top the lamb with the basil. Bake in the oven, and add the potatoes after 30 minutes. Roast for 1 hour 10 minutes.

Let it rest for 10 minutes before serving.

Lamb with Chorizo and Vegetables

Serves 4

1¼ pounds (600 g) fingerling potatoes
4 baby turnips
6 slices spicy cured (Spanish) chorizo
6 fresh chives
6 tablespoons (¾ stick/80 g) butter
A few radishes
2 racks of lamb (2½ pounds/1.2 kg total)
Salt and black pepper

Saucepan
Roasting pan

360°F (180°C) oven

Preparation time: 10 minutes

Cooking time: 40 minutes

Preheat the oven to 360°F (180°C).

Cut the potatoes and turnips in half. Cut the chorizo into matchsticks. Chop the chives. Cut the butter into small pieces. Trim the radishes.

Bring a saucepan of water to a boil. Add the potatoes and turnips and cook for 10 minutes, then drain.

Put the racks of lamb in a roasting pan, season with salt and pepper, and surround them with the potatoes, turnips, radishes, and chorizo. Dot the lamb with butter all over. Bake for 30 minutes.

Sprinkle with the chives before serving.

Lamb with Potatoes and Bay Leaves

Serves 4

1¾ pounds (800 g) Yukon Gold potatoes
4 onions
4 bay leaves
4½ cups (1 L) vegetable stock
Salt and black pepper
8 (3½-ounce/100-g) bone-in lamb
   cutlets

Mandoline
Large baking dish

360°F (180°C) oven

Preparation time: 20 minutes

Cooking time: 45 minutes

Preheat the oven to 360°F (180°C).

Peel the potatoes. Thinly slice the potatoes and onions using a mandoline.

In a large baking dish, make alternating layers of potato and onion, with bay leaves in between.

Season the stock with salt and pepper. Pour the stock into the baking dish (the potatoes should be completely covered). Bake for 30 minutes.

Arrange the cutlets on top of the vegetables, season with salt and pepper, and bake for 15 minutes more, and serve.

Lamb with Artichokes and Mint

Serves 4

3 onions
1 red bell pepper
1 bunch fresh mint
3 tablespoons olive oil
1¾ pounds (800 g) lamb stew meat,
    cubed
1 teaspoon all-purpose flour
2 cups (500 ml) vegetable stock
1 bay leaf
Salt and black pepper
12 artichoke hearts packed in oil,
    drained

Dutch oven

Preparation time: 15 minutes

Cooking time: 3 hours 10 minutes

Slice the onions and bell pepper. Finely chop the mint.

In a Dutch oven, heat the olive oil over medium heat. Add the lamb, onions, and bell pepper and cook, stirring, for 5 minutes. Add the flour and cook for 5 minutes more. Pour in the stock, add the bay leaf, cover, and cook for 1 hour 30 minutes over low heat. Season with salt and black pepper.

Add the artichokes and bake for 1 hour 30 minutes more.

Sprinkle the mint over the top before serving.

Lamb and Dried Fruit Tagine

Serves 4

3 onions
4 cloves garlic
3½ tablespoons (50 g) butter
2 pounds (1 kg) lamb stew meat, cubed
1 teaspoon ground cinnamon
1 teaspoon ground ginger
1 teaspoon grated fresh nutmeg
1 teaspoon coriander seeds
1 teaspoon cumin seeds
1¼ cups (300 ml) chicken stock
¾ cup (100 g) raisins
⅔ cup (100 g) dried apricots
¾ cup (100 g) pitted prunes
⅔ cup (100 g) pitted dates
Salt and black pepper
Handful of arugula

Tagine or Dutch oven

Preparation time: 15 minutes

Cooking time: 1 hour 35 minutes

Coarsely chop the onions and garlic.

In a tagine or Dutch oven, melt the butter over medium heat. Add the lamb, onions, garlic, cinnamon, ginger, nutmeg, coriander, and cumin and cook, stirring, for 5 minutes.

Pour in the stock, add the raisins, apricots, prunes, and dates, and season with salt and pepper. Cover and cook for 1 hour 30 minutes over low heat, checking occasionally and adding a little water if it seems dry.

Top with the arugula before serving.

Maghreb Lamb

Serves 4

1 onion
6 cloves garlic
2 ripe tomatoes
1 stalk celery
2 medium carrots
2 zucchini
3 tablespoons olive oil
1¾ pounds (800 g) lamb shoulder,
 cut into pieces
1 teaspoon ground cinnamon
1 teaspoon ras el hanout
1 teaspoon ground ginger
½ teaspoon grated nutmeg
3 tablespoons tomato paste

1 teaspoon harissa paste
¾ cup (100 g) sultanas (yellow raisins)
Salt
1½ cups (250 g) canned chickpeas,
 drained and rinsed
Leaves from 1 bunch fresh cilantro

Dutch oven

320°F (160°C) oven

Preparation time: 10 minutes

Cooking time: 2 hours 10 minutes

Preheat the oven to 320°F (160°C).

Finely chop the onion and garlic. Small dice the tomatoes. Chop the celery. Quarter the carrots and zucchini lengthwise, then cut them crosswise into 2-inch (5-cm) sticks.

In a Dutch oven, heat the olive oil over medium heat. Add the lamb, garlic, and onion and cook, stirring, until golden brown. Add the cinnamon, ras el hanout, ginger, and nutmeg and lightly brown them.

Pour in enough water to cover the ingredients by about 2 inches (5 cm), then add the tomato paste, harissa, carrots, raisins, and celery and season with salt. Cover and bake for 1 hour 30 minutes.

Uncover the dish and add the zucchini, chickpeas, and cilantro. Bake for 30 minutes more, before serving.

Lamb with Beans and Thyme

Serves 4

2 onions
3 medium carrots
3 tablespoons olive oil
4 (14-ounce/400-g) lamb shanks
   (preferably hind shanks)
7 ounces (200 g) dried navy beans
   or other white beans
1¼ cups (300 ml) white wine
2½ cups (600 ml) vegetable stock
1 teaspoon dried thyme
5 cloves garlic, unpeeled
Salt and black pepper

Dutch oven

390°F (200°C) oven
then 320°F (160°C)

Preparation time: 10 minutes

Cooking time: 2 hours 5 minutes

Preheat the oven to 390°F (200°C).

Chop the onions and dice the carrots.

In a Dutch oven, heat the olive oil over medium heat. Add the onions and carrots and cook, stirring, for 5 minutes. Add the lamb and cook until browned. Transfer the pot to the oven and roast for 15 minutes.

Reduce the oven temperature to 320°F (160°C). Add the beans and pour in the wine and stock. Add the thyme and garlic, season with salt and pepper, cover, and bake for 1 hour.

Remove the lid and bake for 45 minutes more, checking occasionally to make sure the pot isn't drying out (add a little water if necessary), and then serve.

Lamb with Fruit and Nuts

Serves 4

4 onions
4 (14-ounce/400-g) lamb shanks,
  preferably hind shanks
1 cup (150 g) dried apricots
1 cup plus 2 tablespoons (150 g)
  pitted prunes
2 cups (500 ml) chicken stock
Salt and black pepper
1 teaspoon ground cinnamon
1 teaspoon ground ginger
¾ cup (100 g) unsalted cashews

Dutch oven

320°F (160°C) oven

Preparation time: 5 minutes

Cooking time: 2 hours

Preheat the oven to 320°F (160°C).

 Cut the onions into wedges.

Place the shanks in a Dutch oven and add the onions, apricots, and prunes. Pour in the stock and season with salt and pepper. Stir in the cinnamon and ginger, cover, and bake for 2 hours.

Add the cashews before serving.

Alsatian Baker's Stew

Serves 4

14 ounces (400 g) pork neck or shoulder
10½ ounces (300 g) lamb shoulder
7 ounces (200 g) beef shank
3 cloves garlic
2 bay leaves
Leaves from 2 sprigs fresh thyme
2 pounds (1 kg) potatoes
2 onions
2 medium carrots
6 tablespoons (¾ stick/80 g) butter
Salt and black pepper
2½ cups (600 ml) dry Riesling wine

Mandoline
Dutch oven

360°F (180°C) oven

Preparation time: 20 minutes

Cooking time: 2 hours

Preheat the oven to 360°F (180°C).

Cut the pork, lamb, and beef into small ½-inch (1-cm) cubes and put them in a bowl. Chop the garlic with the bay leaves and thyme leaves, then mix them with the meat. Peel the potatoes. Thinly slice the potatoes, onions, and carrots on a mandoline.

Butter a Dutch oven. Make alternating layers of the potatoes, onions, carrots, and meat, ending with a layer of potatoes and seasoning each layer with salt and pepper. Pour the Riesling over the layers, cover, and bake for 2 hours; the casserole must remain tightly sealed for the duration of the cooking time.

Serve immediately.

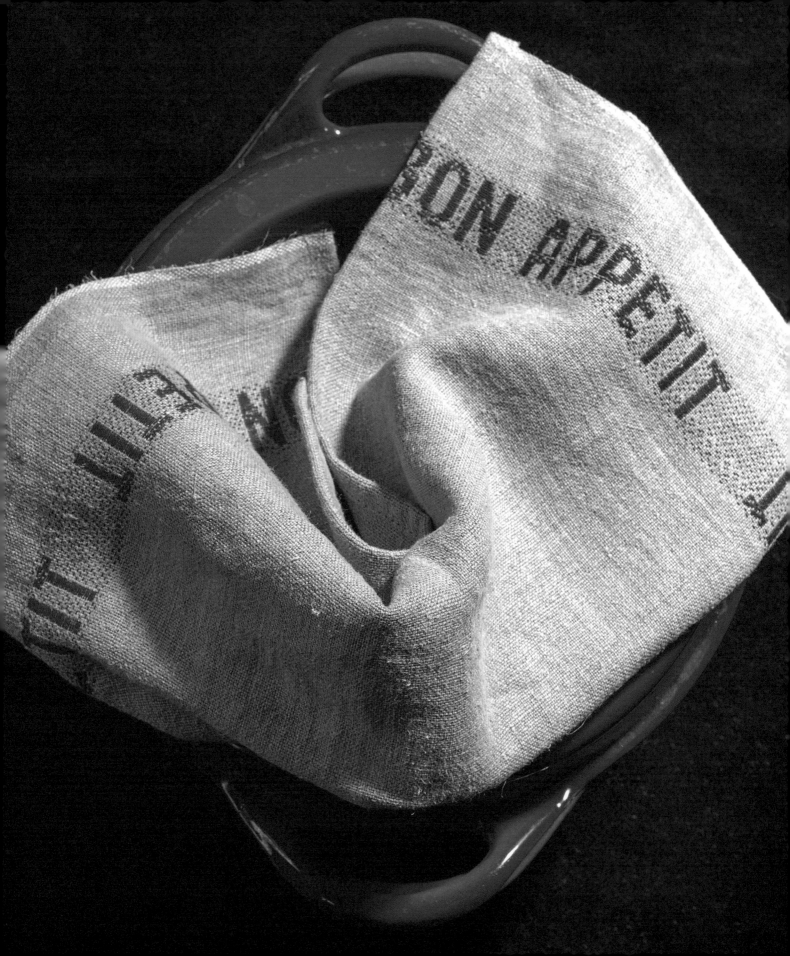

Chicken with Cilantro and Green Vegetables

Serves 4

4 spring onions
1 pound (500 g) fresh peas
1 bunch thin green asparagus
1 zucchini
1 bunch fresh cilantro
3 tablespoons olive oil
1 (3-pound/1.4-kg) chicken, cut into
   8 pieces
3 cups (700 ml) chicken stock
Salt and black pepper

Dutch oven

Preparation time: 15 minutes

Cooking time: 50 minutes

Quarter the bulbs of the spring onions and slice the stems into 2-inch (5-cm) pieces. Shell the peas. Peel the asparagus into strips using a vegetable peeler. Large dice the zucchini. Remove the leaves from the cilantro and coarsely chop them; tie the stems into a bundle with kitchen twine.

In a Dutch oven, heat the olive oil over medium heat. Add the onion bulbs and cook, stirring, for 2 minutes. Add the cilantro stems and the chicken, pour in the stock, and season with salt and pepper.

Simmer for 40 minutes, then add the peas, asparagus, zucchini, and onion stems. Cook for 5 minutes more.

Remove the cilantro stems and add the leaves before serving.

Coq au Vin

Serves 4

5¼ ounces (150 g) mushrooms
4 cloves garlic
4 shallots
2 medium carrots
3½ ounces (100 g) thick-cut bacon,
    cut into lardons
3 tablespoons olive oil
1 free-range (3-pound/1.4-kg) chicken,
    cut into 8 pieces (long live butchers!)
1 tablespoon all-purpose flour
3 tablespoons (50 ml) cognac
1 teaspoon herbes de Provence
2 cups (500 ml) Rhône Valley red wine
1⅔ cups (400 ml) veal stock
Salt and black pepper

Dutch oven

Preparation time: 20 minutes

Cooking time: 1 hour 50 minutes

Quarter the mushrooms. Crush the garlic. Halve the shallots. Slice the carrots into rounds.

In a Dutch oven over medium heat, cook the bacon until the fat has rendered out. Remove it with a slotted spoon and set aside. Add the olive oil and the chicken, working in batches, if necessary, and brown the chicken. Return the bacon to the pot and add the shallots and garlic. Sprinkle with the flour and cook for 5 minutes.

Add the cognac and using a long kitchen match or barbecue lighter, very carefully flambé it. When the flames have cooked off, add the vegetables and herbes de Provence. Pour in the wine and stock and cook, uncovered, over low heat for 1 hour 30 minutes.

Season with salt and pepper before serving.

MEAT

Chicken with Lemon and Peas

Serves 4

1 bunch asparagus
2 organic onions
2 organic unwaxed lemons
1 pound (500 g) fresh peas
1 (3-pound/1.4-kg) chicken, cut into
    8 pieces
3 tablespoons olive oil
2 stalks lemongrass
1 teaspoon herbes de Provence
Fine sea salt

Dutch oven or roasting pan

320°F (160°C) oven

Preparation time: 15 minutes

Cooking time: 1 hour

Preheat the oven to 320°F (160°C).

Cut the asparagus into 2½-inch (6-cm) lengths. Cut the onions and lemons into wedges without peeling. Shell the peas.

Arrange the chicken pieces in a Dutch oven or roasting pan, brush with the olive oil, add the onions, lemons, lemongrass, and herbes de Provence, and season with salt.

Bake for 45 minutes. Take the pan out of the oven, remove the chicken pieces, add the asparagus, return the chicken to the pan, and bake for 15 minutes more.

Remove the lemongrass before serving.

Chicken and Ratatouille

Serves 4

2 zucchini
4 ripe tomatoes
1 eggplant
2 onions
Leaves from 1 bunch fresh basil
1 (3-pound/1.4-kg) chicken
¼ cup (60 ml) olive oil
4 cloves garlic
3½ ounces (100 g) dry-cured
   black olives, pitted
¾ cup (200 ml) chicken stock
Salt and black pepper

Dutch oven

320°F (160°C) oven

Preparation time: 15 minutes

Cooking time: 1 hour 30 minutes

Preheat the oven to 320°F (160°C).

Medium dice the zucchini, tomatoes, and eggplant. Slice the onions. Slip the basil leaves under the skin of the chicken breasts.

Put the chicken in a Dutch oven, drizzle with the olive oil, and arrange the onions and garlic around the chicken. Bake for 30 minutes.

Add the zucchini, tomatoes, eggplant, olives, and stock, season with salt and pepper, cover, and bake for 1 hour more.

Carve the chicken and then serve.

Chicken with Garam Masala and Coconut

Serves 4

2 onions
4 cloves garlic
1 red chile pepper
3 ripe tomatoes
3 tablespoons olive oil
1 (3-pound/1.4-kg) chicken,
    cut into 8 pieces
1 tablespoon garam masala
¾ cup (200 ml) white wine
1⅔ cups (400 ml) coconut milk
Salt
Leaves from 1 bunch fresh basil
Cooked rice, for serving

Dutch oven

320°F (160°C) oven

Preparation time: 15 minutes

Cooking time: 1 hour

Preheat the oven to 320°F (160°C).

Slice the onions and garlic. Thinly slice the chile. Cut the tomatoes into wedges.

In a Dutch oven, heat the olive oil over medium heat. Add the onions, garlic, and chile and cook, stirring, for 5 minutes.

Add the chicken and garam masala and cook for 5 minutes more, until the chicken is browned. Pour in the wine, then add the tomatoes and coconut milk and season with salt. Cook over low heat for 45 minutes.

Add the basil leaves 5 minutes before serving alongside steamed rice.

Chicken with Sesame Seeds and Sweet Potatoes

Serves 4

4 onions
4 sweet potatoes
1 (3-pound/1.4-kg) chicken
3 tablespoons sweet soy sauce
   (kecap manis)
Fine sea salt
1 tablespoon sesame seeds
Black pepper
3 tablespoons olive oil

Baking dish

320°F (160°C) oven

Preparation time: 10 minutes

Cooking time: 1 hour 15 minutes

Preheat the oven to 320°F (160°C).

Cut the onions into wedges. Peel and large dice the sweet potatoes.

Put the chicken in a baking dish. Drizzle with the soy sauce and sprinkle with salt and the sesame seeds. Surround the chicken with the sweet potatoes and onions, season with salt and pepper, drizzle with the olive oil, and bake for 1 hour 15 minutes. Stir the vegetables at regular intervals to make sure they bake evenly.

Carve the chicken and then serve.

Chicken with Blood Oranges

Serves 4

2 onions
4 organic unwaxed blood oranges
1 (3-pound/1.4-kg) chicken
3 tablespoons olive oil
Fine sea salt and cracked pepper

Baking dish

320°F (160°C) oven

Preparation time: 5 minutes

Cooking time: 1 hour 15 minutes

Preheat the oven to 320°F (160°C).

Slice the onions. Cut 2 unpeeled oranges into eighths. Zest and juice the remaining 2 oranges.

Put the chicken in a baking dish. Brush with the olive oil, season with salt and pepper, and sprinkle with the orange zest.

Arrange the sliced onions and orange wedges around the chicken. Pour the orange juice over the chicken and onions and bake for 1 hour 15 minutes.

Carve the chicken and then serve.

Poulet au Lait

Serves 4

4 onions
3 tablespoons olive oil
1 (3-pound/1.4-kg) chicken
12 cloves garlic
4½ cups (1 L) whole milk
Salt and black pepper

Dutch oven

320°F (160°C) oven

Preparation time: 15 minutes

Cooking time: 1 hour 5 minutes

Preheat the oven to 320°F (160°C).

Slice the onions.

In a Dutch oven, heat the olive oil over medium heat. Add the onions and cook for 5 minutes. Add the chicken, garlic, and milk; season with salt and pepper. Cover and bake for 1 hour, basting the chicken regularly with the milk.

Carve the chicken and then serve.

Chicken Drumsticks

Serves 4

3 cloves garlic
3 tablespoons olive oil
3 tablespoons ketchup
1 tablespoon ground cumin
1 teaspoon cracked coriander seeds
2 tablespoons sweet soy sauce
   (kecap manis)
12 chicken drumsticks (about 3 pounds/
   1.4 kg)
Several pickled green chiles, drained

Baking dish

360°F (180°C) oven

Preparation time: 10 minutes

Cooking time: 45 minutes

Preheat the oven to 360°F (180°C).

Finely chop the garlic.

In a large bowl, mix together the garlic, olive oil, ketchup, cumin, coriander, and soy sauce. Add the chicken and toss to coat.

Spread out the drumsticks in a baking dish with the marinade. Bake for 45 minutes.

Top with the chiles before serving.

Rabbit with Artichokes and Fennel Seeds

Serves 4

3 onions
10½ ounces (300 g) oil-packed
    artichoke hearts, drained
1 (3-pound/1.4-kg) rabbit, cut into
    8 pieces
1 tablespoon fennel seeds
3 tablespoons olive oil
¾ cup (200 ml) white wine
Salt and black pepper
Leaves from a few sprigs fresh flat-leaf parsley

Baking dish

320°F (160°C) oven

Preparation time: 15 minutes

Cooking time: 45 minutes

Preheat the oven to 320°F (160°C).

Thinly slice the onions. Slice the artichoke hearts.

Put the rabbit in a baking dish, add the artichokes and onions, and sprinkle with the fennel seeds. Drizzle with the olive oil and pour in the wine. Season with salt and pepper. Bake for 45 minutes.

Scatter with parsley leaves before serving.

Rabbit with Lemon Thyme and Almonds

Serves 4

2 onions
2 tablespoons olive oil
1 (3-pound/1.4-kg) rabbit, cut into 8 pieces
1 teaspoon all-purpose flour
1¼ cups (300 ml) chicken stock
1 bunch fresh lemon thyme
¾ cup (100 g) unsalted blanched
    whole almonds
Salt and pepper
1¼ cups (300 ml) heavy cream

Dutch oven

Preparation time: 15 minutes

Cooking time: 45 minutes

Slice the onions.

In a Dutch oven, heat the olive oil over medium heat. Add the rabbit and onions and cook, stirring.

Add the flour and let it brown for 5 minutes. Pour in the stock. Add the lemon thyme sprigs and the almonds. Season with salt and pepper and cook, covered, for 30 minutes over low heat.

Add the cream and cook, uncovered, for 10 minutes more, and then serve immediately.

MEAT

Rabbit Lyonnais

Serves 4

4 onions
6 ripe tomatoes
4 cloves garlic
1 (3-pound/1.4-kg) rabbit,
　cut into 8 pieces
Salt and black pepper
8 slices thick-cut bacon
Leaves from 1 sprig fresh rosemary
Leaves from 2 sprigs fresh thyme
¾ cup (200 ml) white wine
⅔ cup (150 ml) olive oil

Dutch oven

360°F (180°C) oven

Preparation time: 15 minutes

Cooking time: 45 minutes

Preheat the oven to 360°F (180°C).

Slice the onions and tomatoes. Crush the garlic.

Make a layer of tomatoes and onions in a Dutch oven, place the rabbit on top, and season with salt and pepper. Top with the bacon, rosemary leaves, and thyme leaves. Season with salt and pepper, add the wine, and pour the olive oil over the top. Cover and bake for 30 minutes.

Remove the lid and bake for 15 minutes more, and then serve.

Rabbit with Pine Nuts and Cinnamon

Serves 4

4 shallots
3 ripe tomatoes
1 slice thick-cut bacon
3 tablespoons olive oil
1 teaspoon ground cinnamon
1 (3-pound/1.4-kg) rabbit, jointed
3 bay leaves
2 cups (500 ml) chicken stock
2 tablespoons tomato paste
1 tablespoon harissa paste
2 cinnamon sticks
⅓ cup (50 g) pine nuts
Salt

Dutch oven

Preparation time: 10 minutes

Cooking time: 50 minutes

Slice the shallots. Chop the tomatoes. Cut the bacon into lardons.

In a Dutch oven, heat the olive oil over medium heat. Add the shallots, bacon, and ground cinnamon and cook for 5 minutes. Add the rabbit, bay leaves, and tomatoes. Pour in the stock. Add the tomato paste, harissa, and cinnamon sticks, then the pine nuts. Season with salt and cook for 45 minutes over low heat.

Remove the cinnamon sticks before serving.

Sunday Night Pasta

Serves 4

14 ounces (400 g) leftover roast meat
    (lamb, pork . . .)
7 ounces (200 g) dried trofie (Ligurian
    twisted pasta) or gemelli
1 cup (200 g) leftover cooked vegetables (peas,
    ratatouille . . .)
Salt and black pepper
1¼ cups (300 ml) vegetable stock
3½ ounces (100 g) grated cheese

Baking dish

360°F (180°C) oven

Preparation time: 10 minutes

Cooking time: 10 minutes

Preheat the oven to 360°F (180°C).

Chop the meat into small cubes and put it in a bowl. Add the dried pasta and leftover vegetables and toss to combine. Season with salt and pepper.

Transfer the mixture to a baking dish, cover with the stock, sprinkle with the cheese, and bake for 10 minutes, until the pasta is al dente.

Serve immediately.

Fish and More

Salmon with Beets and Chocolate Mint

Serves 4

1 (1¾-pound/800-g) skin-on salmon fillet,
  pin bones removed
2 beets
3 slices smoked salmon (2¾ to 3½ ounces/
  80 to 100 g each)
2 spring onions
1 stalk lemongrass
Juice of 1 lemon
1 tablespoon sugar
2 tablespoons fish sauce
3 tablespoons olive oil
1 bunch fresh chocolate mint

Baking dish

210°F (100°C) oven

Preparation time: 15 minutes

Cooking time: 20 minutes

Preheat the oven to 210°F (100°C).

Lay the salmon fillet in a baking dish, skin side down, and bake for
20 minutes.

Peel and slice the beets. Slice the smoked salmon into strips. Slice the
spring onions. Finely chop the lemongrass.

In a small bowl, mix together the lemon juice, sugar, fish sauce, and olive
oil to make a vinaigrette.

As soon as the salmon comes out of the oven, cover it with the raw beets,
smoked salmon, onions, and lemongrass, drizzle with the vinaigrette,
and scatter with the chocolate mint. Serve immediately.

Salmon with Baby Vegetables and Olives

Serves 4

1 bunch multicolored baby carrots
1 bunch red radishes
2 shallots
¾ cup (200 ml) vegetable stock
1 teaspoon fennel seeds
4 (6¼- to 7-ounce/200-g) skin-on
   salmon fillets
⅓ cup (50 g) pitted black olives
3 tablespoons olive oil
Salt and black pepper

Saucepan
Baking dish

210°F (100°C) oven

Preparation time: 15 minutes

Cooking time: 30 minutes

Preheat the oven to 210°F (100°C).

Trim the carrots and radishes, leaving some green tops.

Bring a saucepan of salted water to a boil. Add the carrots and radishes and cook for 10 minutes. Drain. Finely chop the shallots and put them in a small bowl. Add the stock and fennel seeds and stir to combine.

Pour the shallot mixture into a baking dish. Lay the salmon on top, flesh side down, and add the carrots, radishes, and olives. Drizzle with the olive oil and season with salt and pepper.

Cover with aluminum foil and bake for 20 minutes, and then serve.

Scallops and Shrimp with Peanuts

Serves 4

2 onions
⅓ cup (50 g) unsalted peanuts
3 tablespoons olive oil
7 ounces (200 g) shelled fresh peas
1 teaspoon curry powder
8 large shrimp, peeled and deveined
8 large scallops
6 tablespoons (100 ml) fish stock
6 tablespoons (100 ml) coconut milk
Salt and black pepper
Leaves from 2 sprigs fresh flat-leaf parsley

Dutch oven

Preparation time: 10 minutes

Cooking time: 15 minutes

Cut the onions into wedges. Coarsely crush the peanuts.

In a Dutch oven, heat the olive oil over medium heat. Add the onions, peas, and curry powder and cook, stirring.

Add the shrimp and scallops, pour in the stock and coconut milk, and cook for 5 minutes, just until the shrimp turn pink. Season with salt and pepper.

Top with the peanuts and parsley before serving.

Scallops with Ham and Sauternes

Serves 4

2 sweet onions, unpeeled
2 slices (2 ounces/55g) Bayonne ham or other
   cured ham
3 golden turnips
2 sprigs fresh dill
1⅔ cups (400 ml) vegetable stock
6 tablespoons (100 ml) Sauternes wine
4 cloves garlic
12 large scallops
6 tablespoons (¾ stick/80 g) butter

Dutch oven

Preparation time: 10 minutes

Cooking time: 20 minutes

Cut the onions into wedges. Thinly slice the ham. Peel the turnips and cut them into thin wedges. Chop the dill.

In a Dutch oven, combine the stock and Sauternes. Add the turnips, onions, garlic, and ham and cook over medium-low heat for 15 minutes. Add the scallops and butter and cook for 5 minutes more, just until the scallops are cooked through.

Scatter with the dill before serving.

Mussels with Chorizo and Cream

Serves 4

1 large onion
3 cloves garlic
1 tablespoon cornstarch
2½ cups (600 ml) heavy cream
6 slices (1¾ ounces/50 g) spicy cured
   (Spanish) chorizo
⅔ cup (150 ml) white wine
¼ cup (½ stick/55 g) butter
8 pounds (3.5 kg) mussels, scrubbed
   and debearded

Dutch oven

Preparation time: 10 minutes

Cooking time: 15 minutes

Finely chop the onion and garlic.

In a small bowl, mix the cornstarch with the cream.

In a Dutch oven, cook the chorizo until it is browned over medium heat. Add the wine, garlic, and onion, then the butter.

Add the mussels, cover, and cook for 5 minutes, then add the cream and cook, uncovered, stirring occasionally, for another 5 minutes.

Discard any mussels that have not opened, before serving.

Shellfish with Butter, Wine, and Star Anise

Serves 4

2 shallots
2 cloves garlic
½ bunch fresh curly parsley
1 fennel bulb
⅔ cup (150 ml) white wine
3 star anise pods
1 cinnamon stick
2 tablespoons balsamic vinegar
6 tablespoons (¾ stick/80 g) butter
4½ pounds (2 kg) mussels, scrubbed
   and debearded
12 razor clams
14 ounces (400 g) clams

Dutch oven

Preparation time: 10 minutes

Cooking time: 10 minutes

Finely chop the shallots and garlic. Chop the parsley. Slice the fennel.

In a Dutch oven, combine the wine, garlic, shallots, fennel, star anise, and cinnamon. Bring to a boil and simmer for 5 minutes.

Add the vinegar and butter, then the shellfish, and cook for 5 minutes more.

Discard any clams or mussels that do not open. Scatter the parsley over the top before serving.

Rice with Cuttlefish Ink and Shellfish

Serves 4

4 packets (½ ounce/14 g total) cuttlefish ink
   (purchase from your fishmonger)
1⅔ cups (400 ml) fish stock
2 shallots
3 calamari, prepared by your fishmonger
¼ cup (60 ml) olive oil
1 heaping cup (200 g) basmati rice
2 pounds (1 kg) mussels, scrubbed
   and debearded
12 razor clams
3 sprigs fresh dill
1 lemon, halved
Salt and black pepper

Dutch oven or flameproof baking dish

360°F (180°C) oven

Preparation time: 15 minutes

Cooking time: 20 minutes

Preheat the oven to 360°F (180°C).

In a small bowl, mix the cuttlefish ink with the stock. Finely chop the shallots. Slice the calamari into rings.

In a Dutch oven or flameproof baking dish, heat the olive oil over high heat. Add the shallots and calamari and cook briefly, stirring. Add the rice and cook, stirring, for a few moments, until it is translucent. Pour in the stock and nestle the shellfish in the rice. Cover with parchment paper and bake for 15 minutes.

Top with torn sprigs of dill and a squeeze of the lemon halves and season with salt and pepper before serving.

Seafood with Ginger and Cilantro

Serves 4

2 ounces (50 g) fresh ginger
2 shallots
Pinch of saffron
1 bunch fresh cilantro
2 calamari, prepared by your fishmonger
¾ cup (200 ml) dry white wine
6 tablespoons (¾ stick/80 g) butter
8 large shrimp, peeled and deveined
1 pound (500 g) mussels, scrubbed
   and debearded
12 razor clams
12 clams

Dutch oven

Preparation time: 10 minutes

Cooking time: 10 minutes

Peel and thinly slice the ginger. Slice the shallots. Chop the cilantro. Slice the calamari into rings.

In a Dutch oven, combine the wine, ginger, saffron, and shallots and bring to a boil. Reduce the heat to medium and simmer until the liquid has reduced by half.

Add the butter, then all the seafood and cook for 5 minutes, just until the shrimp are pink.

Discard any clams or mussels that do not open. Scatter with the cilantro before serving.

Seafood Stew

Serves 4

2 shallots
1 bunch radishes
2 tablespoons olive oil
12 vine-ripened cherry tomatoes
8 large shrimp, peeled and deveined
14 ounces (400 g) calamari rings
6 tablespoons (100 ml) white wine
¾ cup (200 ml) heavy cream
Salt and black pepper
Juice of 1 lemon

Dutch oven

Preparation time: 10 minutes

Cooking time: 15 minutes

Finely chop the shallots. Trim the radish tops.

In a Dutch oven, heat the olive oil over medium heat. Add the shallots and cook, stirring, for 2 minutes.

Add the radishes, tomatoes, and seafood and cook for 5 minutes. Add the wine and cook for 5 minutes more, then add the cream and season with salt and pepper.

Add the lemon juice just before serving.

Drumfish, Shrimp, and Calamari

Serves 4

2 shallots
2 calamari, prepared by your fishmonger
2 tablespoons olive oil
4 (6½-ounce/180-g) drumfish fillets (also called
   meager, shadefish, or corvina, but any white
   fish will do)
4 large shrimp, peeled and deveined
6 tablespoons (100 ml) white wine
¾ cup (200 ml) fish stock
1¾ cups (200 g) drained oil-packed
   sun-dried tomatoes
Leaves from 1 bunch fresh basil

Dutch oven

Preparation time: 10 minutes

Cooking time: 15 minutes

Finely chop the shallots. Slice the calamari into rings.

In a Dutch oven, heat the olive oil over medium heat. Add the shallots, fish fillets, shrimp, and calamari. Add the wine and stock, then add the sun-dried tomatoes. Cook for 10 minutes over low heat, just until the shrimp are pink.

Add the basil leaves, stir, and serve.

Cod with Sesame and Zucchini

Serves 4

4 zucchini
2 red onions
1 bunch fresh dill
1 teaspoon fine sea salt
3 tablespoons sesame seeds
4 center-cut cod fillets
6 tablespoons (100 ml) olive oil

Baking dish
390°F (200°C) oven
Preparation time: 15 minutes
Cooking time: 15 minutes

Preheat the oven to 390°F (200°C).

Using a vegetable peeler, peel the zucchini into strips (until you reach the core). Discard the core. Slice the onions into rings. Coarsely chop the dill.

In a small bowl, mix the salt and sesame seeds together.

Lay the onion rings in the bottom of a baking dish. Place the fish fillets on top and sprinkle with the sesame mixture and dill. Arrange the zucchini strips on top and drizzle with the olive oil.

Cover with aluminum foil and bake for 15 minutes, just until the fish begins to flake. Serve immediately.

Salt Cod with Potatoes and Onions

Serves 4

3 red onions
8 baby potatoes
4 salt cod fillets, desalted (see Note)
1 bunch fresh lemon thyme
4 bay leaves
⅔ cup (150 ml) olive oil

Saucepan
Baking dish

360°F (180°C) oven

Preparation time: 10 minutes

Cooking time: 50 minutes

Preheat the oven to 360°F (180°C).

Slice the onions into rings.

Bring a saucepan of water to a boil. Add the potatoes and cook for 20 minutes; they should stay firm. Drain and halve the potatoes.

Lay the fillets in a baking dish, add the potatoes, and scatter with the onions, thyme sprigs, and bay leaves. Drizzle generously with the olive oil and bake for 20 minutes.

Cover with aluminum foil and bake for 10 minutes more, until the fish is tender. Serve immediately.

Note: To remove the salt from salt cod, first rinse the fillets under running water to remove superficial salt. Transfer the cod to a bowl of cold water and let soak in the refrigerator for 12 hours. Drain and repeat the soaking process three more times, or as needed to remove the saltiness.

Mackerel with Tomatoes and Herbs

Serves 4

3 cloves garlic
2 pounds (1 kg) mixed tomatoes
4 (6½-ounce/180-g) good-looking mackerel, cleaned
1 tablespoon herbes de Provence
6 bay leaves
⅔ cup (150 ml) olive oil
Fine sea salt

Baking dish
320°F (160°C) oven
Preparation time: 10 minutes
Cooking time: 20 minutes

Preheat the oven to 320°F (160°C).

Slice the garlic into rounds. Slice the tomatoes crosswise into rounds. Slash the skin of the mackerel in a few places.

Lay the tomatoes in a baking dish and sprinkle with the garlic. Place the mackerel on top, sprinkle with the herbes de Provence and bay leaves, drizzle with the olive oil, and season with salt.

Bake for 20 minutes, until the fish flakes. Serve immediately.

Sea Bass with Fennel and Lemon

Serves 4

4 baby fennel bulbs
1 shallot
Leaves from 2 sprigs fresh lemon thyme
1 lime
1 (4½-pound/2-kg) sea bass, cut into
   2 fillets (long live fishmongers . . .)
1 tablespoon fennel seeds
6 tablespoons (100 ml) olive oil
Salt and black pepper

Saucepan
Baking dish

300°F (150°C) oven

Preparation time: 10 minutes

Cooking time: 25 minutes

Preheat the oven to 300°F (150°C).

Bring a saucepan of salted water to a boil. Add the fennel and cook for 8 minutes. Immediately drain and rinse them under cold water.

Finely chop the shallot. Coarsely chop the lemon thyme leaves. Halve the lime; coarsely chop one half and slice the other.

In a small bowl, combine the shallot, thyme, and chopped lime.

Put one sea bass fillet in a baking dish, skin side down, and press the shallot mixture on the flesh. Drizzle with olive oil and season with salt and pepper. Lay the other fillet on top of the first, flesh side down, then arrange the lime slices and fennel on top.

Drizzle with olive oil and bake for 15 minutes, until the fish is just cooked through. Serve immediately.

Sea Bass with Herbs in a Salt Crust

Serves 4

1 bunch fresh basil
1 bunch fresh dill
1 (4½-pound/2-kg) sea bass, cleaned
    and left whole
6½ pounds (3 kg) coarse salt
6 tablespoons (100 ml) very good-quality
    olive oil
Steamed potatoes, for serving

Rimmed baking sheet
390°F (200°C) oven
Preparation time: 5 minutes
Cooking time: 35 minutes
Resting time: 10 minutes

Preheat the oven to 390°F (200°C).

Stuff the herbs inside the fish.

Make a layer of the coarse salt on a rimmed baking sheet. Place the sea bass on top, cover it completely with salt, and bake for 35 minutes.

Let it rest for 10 minutes, then break the crust.

Serve the fillets drizzled with the olive oil and with steamed potatoes on the side.

Turbot with Bok Choy and Piri Piri

Serves 4

10½ ounces (300 g) bok choy
4 shallots
2 red chile peppers
2 lemons
1 (3-pound/1.5-kg) turbot, cleaned by
    your fishmonger
¾ cup (200 ml) white wine
¾ cup (200 ml) olive oil
Fine sea salt

Saucepan
Baking dish

360°F (180°C) oven

Preparation time: 10 minutes

Cooking time: 30 minutes

Preheat the oven to 360°F (180°C).

Slice the bok choy crosswise into thick strips. Finely chop the shallots. Chop the chiles. Cut the lemons into wedges.

Bring a saucepan of salted water to a boil. Add the bok choy and cook for 10 minutes, then remove with a slotted spoon and rinse under cold water; reserve the cooking liquid.

Lay the turbot in a baking dish, pour over the wine and olive oil, and scatter with the shallots and chiles. Bake for 20 minutes, until it is flaky.

Reheat the bok choy in the cooking liquid, then spoon it around the fish.

Season with salt and serve with the lemon wedges.

Cod with Peppers and Chorizo

Serves 4

2 red bell peppers
1 green bell pepper
1 red onion
3½ ounces (100 g) spicy cured (Spanish)
   chorizo
6 tablespoons (100 ml) olive oil
1 (1¾-pound/800-g) cod fillet
Fine sea salt

Baking dish

320°F (160°C) oven

Preparation time: 10 minutes

Cooking time: 20 minutes

Preheat the oven to 320°F (160°C).

Thinly slice the bell peppers. Slice the onion. Cut the chorizo into matchsticks.

In a medium bowl, mix the onions, bell peppers, and chorizo with the olive oil.

Lay the cod in a baking dish, cover with the chorizo mixture, and bake for 20 minutes, until the fish is flaky.

Season with salt before serving.

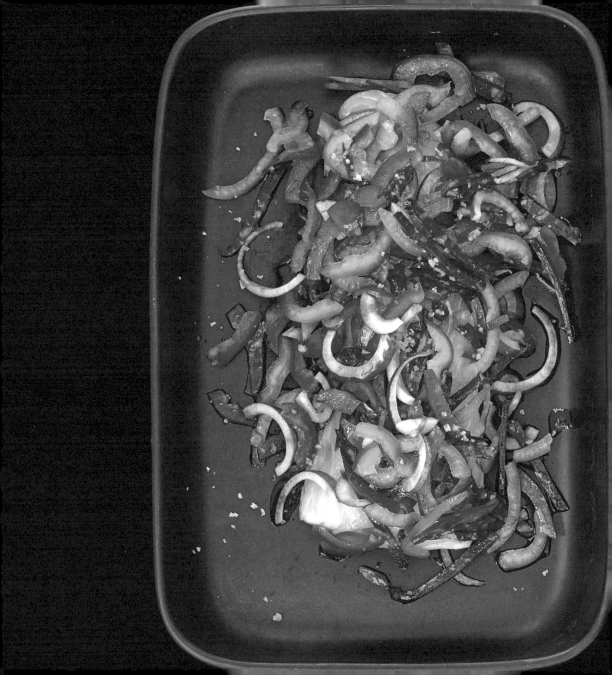

Cod with Coconut and Lemon

Serves 4

1 lemon
1 zucchini
4 baby carrots
1 cup (250 ml) coconut milk
4 (6½-ounce/180-g) cod fillets
1 teaspoon fennel seeds
Salt and black pepper
2 sprigs fresh dill

Dutch oven

Preparation time: 10 minutes

Cooking time: 15 minutes

Zest and juice the lemon. Cut the zucchini into sticks. Trim the tops of the carrots to about 1 inch (2.5 cm) and quarter the carrots lengthwise.

In a small bowl, mix the coconut milk with the lemon juice.

Lay the cod fillets in a Dutch oven and top with the zucchini, carrots, and lemon zest. Cover with the lemon coconut milk, add the fennel seeds, and season with salt and pepper. Cover and cook for 15 minutes over medium-low heat, until the fish is flaky.

Scatter with the sprigs of dill before serving.

Eggs

Eggs with Asparagus and Comté

Serves 4

4 spears green asparagus
3 ounces (80 g) Comté cheese
2 cups (500 ml) heavy cream
Pinch of grated fresh nutmeg
Salt and cracked black pepper
6 fresh chives
4 eggs

Dutch oven or 4 ramekins
Roasting pan

390°F (200°C) oven

Preparation time: 5 minutes

Cooking time: 7–10 minutes

Preheat the oven to 390°F (200°C).

Thinly slice the asparagus crosswise. Dice the cheese. Season the cream with the nutmeg and salt and pepper to taste. Chop the chives.

Crack the eggs into a Dutch oven, or put one in each ramekin and add the asparagus and cheese. Pour the cream over the top.

Set the Dutch oven or ramekins in a roasting pan and place them in the oven. Carefully pour in hot water to come halfway up the side(s) of the Dutch oven (or ramekins) to make a bain-marie. Bake for 7 to 10 minutes, or until the eggs are soft-set.

Remove the dish(es) from the bain-marie. Sprinkle with the chives and serve immediately.

Eggs with Salmon

Serves 4

4 (6½-ounce/180-g) slices smoked salmon
2 cups (500 ml) heavy cream
Salt and pepper
4 eggs
2 tablespoons salmon roe
3 sprigs fresh cilantro

Dutch oven or 4 ramekins
Roasting pan

390°F (200°C) oven

Preparation time: 5 minutes

Cooking time: 7–10 minutes

Preheat the oven to 390°F (200°C).

Slice the smoked salmon into strips. Season the cream with salt and pepper.

Crack the eggs into a Dutch oven, or put one in each ramekin and add the smoked salmon. Pour the cream over the top.

Set the Dutch oven or ramekins in a roasting pan and place them in the oven. Carefully pour in hot water to come halfway up the side(s) of the Dutch oven (or ramekins) to make a bain-marie. Bake for 7 to 10 minutes, or until the eggs are soft-set.

Remove the dish(es) from the bain-marie. Sprinkle with the salmon roe and cilantro leaves before serving.

Eggs with Morels and Mascarpone

Serves 4

1 ounce (30 g) dried morel mushrooms
2 cups (500 ml) heavy cream
3½ ounces (100 g) mascarpone cheese
Salt and black pepper
4 eggs
Leaves from 3 sprigs fresh flat-leaf parsley

Saucepan
Dutch oven or 4 ramekins
Roasting pan

390°F (200°C) oven

Preparation time: 5 minutes

Cooking time: 25 minutes

Preheat the oven to 390°F (200°C).

Bring a saucepan of water to a boil. Put the mushrooms in a small bowl and pour over boiling water to cover. Set aside to rehydrate for 5 minutes. Drain the mushrooms.

In a Dutch oven, heat the cream over medium heat. Add the mushrooms, reduce the heat to low, and cook for 15 minutes. Let cool, then stir in the mascarpone and season with salt and pepper.

Crack the eggs into the Dutch oven, or put one in each ramekin and pour the morel cream over the top.

Set the Dutch oven or ramekins in a roasting pan and place them in the oven. Carefully pour in hot water to come halfway up the side(s) of the Dutch oven (or ramekins) to make a bain-marie. Bake for 7 to 10 minutes, or until the eggs are soft-set.

Remove the Dutch oven or ramekins from the bain-marie and scatter with the parsley before serving.

Eggs with Sorrel and Sesame

Serves 4

4 fresh sorrel leaves
2 cups (500 ml) heavy cream
Salt and black pepper
4 eggs
1 tablespoon sesame seeds
1 tablespoon sesame oil

Dutch oven or 4 ramekins
Roasting pan

390°F (200°C) oven

Preparation time: 5 minutes

Cooking time: 7–10 minutes

Preheat the oven to 390°F (200°C).

Shred the sorrel. Season the cream with salt and pepper.

Crack the eggs into the Dutch oven, or put one in each ramekin and add the sorrel. Pour the cream over the top.

Set the Dutch oven or ramekins in a roasting pan and place them in the oven. Carefully pour in hot water to come halfway up the side(s) of the Dutch oven (or ramekins) to make a bain-marie. Bake for 7 to 10 minutes, or until the eggs are soft-set.

Remove the Dutch oven or ramekins from the bain-marie. Sprinkle with the sesame seeds and drizzle with the sesame oil.

Veggies

Asparagus with Nori and Roquefort

Serves 4

3 sheets nori seaweed
1 bunch green asparagus
3½ ounces (100 g) Roquefort cheese
2 cups (500 ml) vegetable stock
7 ounces (200 g) frozen fava beans
2 ounces (50 g) croutons

Dutch oven

Preparation time: 10 minutes

Cooking time: 5 minutes

Shred the nori. Trim the ends of the asparagus and cut them into 2½-inch (6-cm) lengths. Dice the Roquefort.

Bring the stock to a boil in a Dutch oven. Add the asparagus, fava beans, nori, and Roquefort, and simmer for 3 to 5 minutes, until the beans are al dente.

Add the croutons and serve.

Peas with Tofu and Wonton Strips

Serves 4

7 ounces (200 g) organic firm tofu
2 pounds (1 kg) fresh peas
6 wonton wrappers
2 cups (500 ml) vegetable stock
1 bunch shiso leaves

Dutch oven

Preparation time: 5 minutes

Cooking time: 5 minutes

Cut the tofu into cubes. Shell the peas. Slice the wonton wrappers into thick strips.

In a Dutch oven, bring the stock to a boil. Add the peas, tofu, and wonton strips. Simmer for 5 minutes, until heated through.

Add the shiso leaves and serve.

Parsnips, Beets, and Turnips Baked in Salt

Serves 4

2 beets, unpeeled
2 golden turnips, unpeeled
2 parsnips, unpeeled
4½ pounds (2 kg) coarse salt
Olive oil

Dutch oven

320°F (160°C) oven

Preparation time: 5 minutes

Cooking time: 1 hour 30 minutes

Preheat the oven to 320°F (160°C).

Scrub the vegetables.

Make a layer of salt in the bottom of a Dutch oven. Put the whole vegetables on top and cover completely with more coarse salt.

Bake for 1 hour 30 minutes, until they are tender. Let them rest for 10 minutes before cracking the salt crust.

Remove the vegetables from the salt crust and brush off any excess salt, if desired. Serve with a drizzle of olive oil.

Fennel and Potatoes with Saffron

Serves 4

14 ounces (400 g) fingerling potatoes
2 onions
3 cups (750 ml) vegetable stock
Pinch of saffron
4 baby fennel bulbs
¾ cup (200 ml) heavy cream
1 egg yolk
Salt and pepper

Dutch oven

Preparation time: 10 minutes

Cooking time: 20 minutes

Halve the fingerling potatoes. Cut the onions into wedges.

In a Dutch oven, heat the stock over medium heat. Add the saffron, onions, and fennel. Cook for 20 minutes, then remove from the heat.

In a small bowl, mix the cream with the egg yolk and pour it into the Dutch oven off the heat; the mixture mustn't boil after this point.

Season with salt and pepper.

Lettuce with Sun-Dried Tomatoes and Mint

Serves 4

8 heads Little Gem lettuce (see Note)
6 tablespoons (¾ stick/80 g) butter
1⅓ cups (150 g) drained oil-packed
    sun-dried tomatoes
2 cups (500 ml) vegetable stock
Salt
1 teaspoon cracked black pepper
12 fresh mint leaves

Baking dish

320°F (160°C) oven

Preparation time: 5 minutes

Cooking time: 20 minutes

Preheat the oven to 320°F (160°C).

Halve the lettuces lengthwise. Cut the butter into small pieces.

Arrange the lettuce halves, cut side up, in a baking dish. Wedge the sun-dried tomatoes between the lettuces and pour in the stock; season with salt and the cracked pepper.

Dot the top with the butter and bake, uncovered, for 15 minutes.

Add the mint leaves, cover with aluminum foil, and bake for 5 minutes more, until the lettuces are tender.

Note: Often described as a cross between butterhead and romaine, this miniature lettuce is uniquely sweet and buttery. If you can't find Little Gem, substitute four to six romaine hearts, cut in half lengthwise.

Red Endive with Orange Butter

Serves 4

8 red endives
2 unwaxed organic oranges
3 tablespoons olive oil
1¼ cups (300 ml) vegetable stock
6 tablespoons (¾ stick/80 g) butter
Salt

Dutch oven

Preparation time: 10 minutes

Cooking time: 20 minutes

Halve the endives lengthwise. Zest one of the oranges and juice them both.

In a Dutch oven, heat the olive oil over medium heat. Add the endives and cook them for 5 minutes, stirring. Pour in the stock and orange juice, season with salt, and add the zest and butter.

Cover and cook over low heat for 15 minutes, until the endives are tender. Serve immediately.

Kale with Goat Cheese and Hazelnuts

Serves 4

14 ounces (400 g) kale
2 sweet onions
3½ ounces (100 g) fresh Sainte-Maure
   goat cheese
Generous ⅓ cup (50 g) hazelnuts
3 tablespoons olive oil
6 tablespoons (100 ml) white port
¾ cup (200 ml) vegetable stock
Salt and black pepper

Baking sheet
Dutch oven

350°F (175°C) oven

Preparation time: 10 minutes

Cooking time: 35 minutes

Preheat the oven to 350°F (175°C).

Coarsely chop the kale. Cut the onions into wedges. Cut the goat cheese into large pieces.

Toast the hazelnuts on a baking sheet for 10 to 15 minutes, until the papery skins begin to flake. Transfer to a clean dish towel and rub vigorously to remove the skins.

In a Dutch oven, heat the olive oil over medium heat. Add the kale and cook, stirring. Pour in the port and stock, add the onions, and season with salt and pepper. Cover and cook for 15 minutes, until the onions are tender.

Add the goat cheese and hazelnuts and cook for 5 minutes more, before serving.

Cauliflower with Lemon Mascarpone

Serves 4

1 lemon
2 spring onions
1 good-looking head cauliflower
6 tablespoons (100 ml) olive oil
¾ cup (200 ml) vegetable stock
1 teaspoon cracked black pepper
Fine sea salt
5¼ ounces (150 g) mascarpone cheese

Dutch oven

360°F (180°C) oven

Preparation time: 10 minutes

Cooking time: 1 hour 15 minutes

Preheat the oven to 360°F (180°C).

Zest and juice the lemon. Thinly slice the spring onions. Remove the leaves from the cauliflower and cut off the stem.

Put the whole cauliflower in a Dutch oven, drizzle with the olive oil, and add the stock. Season with the pepper and salt to taste. Cover and bake for 1 hour.

In a small bowl, mix half the onions with the mascarpone and lemon juice.

Remove the lid of the Dutch oven and bake for 15 minutes more, until the cauliflower is browned.

Serve topped with the mascarpone and sprinkled with the lemon zest and remaining onions.

VEGGIES

Spring Vegetable Stew

Serves 4

7 ounces (200 g) fresh peas
14 ounces (400 g) fingerling potatoes
1 bunch green asparagus
¾ cup (200 ml) vegetable stock
6 tablespoons (¾ stick/80 g)
   cold salted butter
4 cloves garlic, unpeeled
4 spring onions
4 baby turnips
10 radishes

Dutch oven

Preparation time: 15 minutes

Cooking time: 25 minutes

Shell the peas, keeping a few in their pods (but remove the strings). Halve the potatoes and cut the asparagus into short pieces.

In a Dutch oven, heat the vegetable stock over medium heat. Add the cold butter and bring to a boil, then reduce the heat to low. Add the garlic, spring onions, potatoes, and turnips. Cover and cook for 20 minutes.

Add the radishes, peas, and asparagus and cook uncovered for 5 minutes more, until they are al dente.

Vegetables with Anchovies and Parmesan

Serves 4

2 parsnips
4 baby carrots
3 spring onions
1 Hokkaido pumpkin (red kuri squash)
2 ounces (50 g) anchovy fillets
Leaves from 1 bunch fresh basil
4 cloves garlic
⅔ cup (150 ml) white wine
6 tablespoons (100 ml) olive oil
Black pepper
2 ounces (50 g) Parmesan cheese

Baking dish

360°F (180°C) oven

Preparation time: 20 minutes

Cooking time: 40 minutes

Preheat the oven to 360°F (180°C).

Peel the parsnips. Halve the parsnips and carrots lengthwise. Quarter the spring onions. Cut the pumpkin into slices, without peeling. Remove the seeds. Chop half the anchovies with half the basil and transfer them to a large bowl. Add the parsnips, carrots, onions, pumpkin, garlic, wine, and olive oil. Stir to combine. Season with pepper.

Arrange everything in a baking dish and bake for 40 minutes, until the vegetables are just tender.

Shave the cheese with a vegetable peeler.

At serving time, scatter the vegetables with the remaining basil leaves, remaining anchovies, and the shaved cheese.

Veggie Lentils

Serves 4

3 shallots
2 cloves garlic
2 medium carrots
1 zucchini
3 ripe tomatoes
1 bunch fresh flat-leaf parsley
1 cup (200 g) blue-green Puy lentils
⅓ cup (50 g) pitted green olives
⅓ cup (50 g) pitted dry-cured
    black olives
1 tablespoon tomato paste
3 cups (750 ml) vegetable stock
Salt and black pepper

Dutch oven

Preparation time: 10 minutes

Cooking time: 20 minutes

Finely slice the shallots and garlic. Medium dice the carrots, zucchini, and tomatoes. Chop the parsley. Rinse the lentils.

In a Dutch oven, combine the shallots, garlic, carrots, zucchini, tomatoes, parsley, lentils, olives, tomato paste, and stock. Stir to combine. Cook over medium-low heat for 20 minutes, until the lentils and vegetables are tender.

Season with salt and pepper before serving.

Penne with Kale and Chile

Serves 4

3 medium carrots
2 leaves kale
2 spring onions
1 red chile pepper
2½ cups (600 ml) vegetable stock
7 ounces (200 g) dried penne
7 ounces (200 g) shelled fresh
   (or frozen) peas
Salt and black pepper

Dutch oven

Preparation time: 15 minutes

Cooking time: 10 minutes

Dice the carrots. Thinly slice the kale, spring onions, and chile.

In a Dutch oven, bring the stock to a boil. Add all the ingredients and cook covered over medium heat for 10 minutes, or as directed on the pasta package.

Season with salt and pepper before serving.

Hiker's Rice

Serves 4

3 shallots
1 red chile pepper
10 fresh chives
3 tablespoons olive oil
1½ scant cups (250 g) basmati rice
1⅔ cups (400 ml) vegetable stock
Salt
⅓ generous cup (50 g) whole hazelnuts
½ scant cup (50 g) hulled pumpkin seeds
½ scant cup (50 g) pistachios

Dutch oven or flameproof baking dish

390°F (200°C) oven

Preparation time: 10 minutes

Cooking time: 20–25 minutes

Preheat the oven to 390°F (200°C).

Finely chop the shallots, chile, and chives.

In a Dutch oven or flameproof baking dish, heat the olive oil over medium heat. Add the shallots and cook, stirring, until they are translucent. Add the rice and stir for 2 minutes. Pour in the stock, season with salt, and add the hazelnuts, pumpkin seeds, pistachios, and chile.

Cover with a sheet of parchment paper pierced in the middle and bake for 15 to 20 minutes, until it is tender.

Fluff up the rice with a fork and sprinkle with the chives, before serving.

VEGGIES

Rice with Vegetables

Serves 4

2 shallots
6 baby turnips
6 radishes
3 tablespoons olive oil
1 generous cup (200 g) basmati rice
6 cloves garlic, unpeeled
3½ ounces (100 g) shelled peas
12 vine-ripened cherry tomatoes
1⅔ cups (400 ml) vegetable stock
Salt and black pepper

Dutch oven or flameproof baking dish

360°F (180°C) oven

Preparation time: 10 minutes

Cooking time: 30 minutes

Preheat the oven to 360°F (180°C).

Finely chop the shallots. Peel and quarter the turnips. Trim the radishes.

In a Dutch oven or flameproof baking dish, heat the olive oil over medium heat. Add the shallots and cook, stirring, until translucent. Add the rice and stir until translucent. Add the garlic, peas, radishes, and tomatoes, then pour in the stock and season with salt and pepper.

Cover with a sheet of parchment paper pierced in the middle and bake for 20 minutes, until the rice is tender, and then serve.

Tofu with Thai Vegetables

Serves 4

1 bunch baby beets
4 baby carrots
4 spring onions
½ cucumber
5¼ ounces (150 g) smoked tofu
3 tablespoons peanut oil
2 Thai bird chiles
1 tablespoon green peppercorns
¾ cup (200 ml) vegetable stock
12 cherry tomatoes
1 bunch fresh Thai basil
2 tablespoons soy sauce

Dutch oven

Preparation time: 10 minutes

Cooking time: 25 minutes

Peel the beets and carrots then halve them lengthwise. Quarter the bulbs of the spring onions, then slice the stems. Thinly slice the cucumber. Slice the tofu into bite-size cubes.

Bring a Dutch oven full of water to a boil. Add the beets and cook for 10 minutes, then drain. Rinse and dry the pot.

In the dry Dutch oven, heat the peanut oil over medium heat. Add the onion bulbs and carrots and cook, stirring. Add the chiles and green peppercorns, pour in the stock, cover, and cook over medium-low heat for 10 minutes.

Add the beets, onion stems, tofu, tomatoes, basil leaves, and soy sauce and cook for 5 minutes more, before serving.

Chickpea and Carrot Tagine

Serves 4

2 onions
1 organic unwaxed orange
3 tablespoons olive oil
1 bunch baby carrots
1 tablespoon fennel seeds
1¼ cups (300 ml) vegetable stock
1½ cups (250 g) canned chickpeas,
   drained and rinsed
Salt and pepper

Tagine or Dutch oven

Preparation time: 10 minutes

Cooking time: 15 minutes

Chop the onions. Cut the orange into eighths, without peeling it. Trim the carrots.

In a tagine or Dutch oven, heat the olive oil over medium heat. Add the onions and cook until softened. Add the carrots, orange wedges, and fennel seeds, pour in the stock, and cook for 10 minutes.

Add the chickpeas and cook for 5 minutes more. Season with salt and pepper.

VEGGIES

Ultimate Savory Tomato Tart

Serves 4

3 ripe heirloom tomatoes
½ medium red onion
3 tablespoons olive oil
1 large disk or sheet frozen puff pastry,
    thawed
1 tablespoon herbes de Provence
2 tablespoons bulgur (optional)
5¼ ounces (150 g) leftover cheese
Fine sea salt

Baking sheet

400°F (205°C) oven

Preparation time: 20 minutes

Cooking time: 30–40 minutes

Preheat the oven to 400°F (205°C).

Slice the tomatoes into thin rounds. Slice the onion, put it in a bowl, and mix with the olive oil.

Unroll the puff pastry on a baking sheet, keeping its parchment paper backing underneath. Lift the pastry up and sprinkle the herbes de Provence underneath. Prick the pastry all over with a fork. Bake for 10 minutes, until lightly puffed.

Remove from the oven and sprinkle the bulgur over the surface, if using, then carefully arrange the tomatoes in a rosette pattern over the pastry. Lay the onions on top of the tomatoes, drizzle with any olive oil remaining in the bowl, top with shavings of the cheese, and season with salt. Bake for 20 to 30 minutes more, until the cheese has melted.

Slice and serve immediately.

Cheese

Fourme d'Ambert with Nuts and Honey

Serves 4

¼ cup (30 g) chopped hazelnuts
¼ cup (30 g) shelled pistachios
¼ cup (30 g) chopped walnuts
1½ teaspoons fennel seeds
A generous 2½ tablespoons (50 g)
   wildflower honey
10½ ounces (300 g) Fourme d'Ambert
   blue cheese (semi-hard cow's-milk cheese)
Country-style bread

⏲ Preparation time: 5 minutes

In a small bowl, mix together all the ingredients except the cheese and bread. Slice and toast the bread.

Serve the cheese with the toast and top with the nut-and-honey mixture.

Picodon with Radish and Arugula

Serves 4

🕐 Preparation time: 5 minutes

6 radishes
1 bunch fresh chives
Handful of arugula
3 tablespoons olive oil
1 teaspoon cracked black pepper
2 Picodon cheeses (soft-rind goat cheese)
Fruit and nut bread, sliced and toasted

Chop the radishes, chives, and arugula. Put the vegetables in a bowl and stir in the olive oil. Season with the pepper.

Serve with the Picodon cheeses and toasted bread.

Saint-Marcellin with Bacon and Peanuts

Serves 4

1 red onion
4 thin slices bacon
⅓ cup (50 g) unsalted peanuts
2 Saint-Marcellin cheeses (soft-rind
   cow's-milk cheese)

Skillet

Preparation time: 5 minutes

Cooking time: 5 minutes

Chop the onion. Cut the bacon into matchsticks.

In a skillet, sauté the bacon and onion for 5 minutes. Add the peanuts and stir.

Serve with the Saint-Marcellin cheeses.

Sainte-Maure with Tomatoes and Spring Onions

Serves 4

⏱ Preparation time: 10 minutes

2 ripe tomatoes
6 fresh chives
1 spring onion
1 stalk celery
¼ cup (60 ml) olive oil
Fine sea salt
1 Sainte-Maure goat cheese
Baguette, sliced and toasted

Dice the tomatoes and finely chop the chives, the spring onion with its stem, and the celery. Put the vegetables in a bowl and mix in the olive oil; season with salt.

Serve the vegetables with the Sainte-Maure on toast.

Tomme de Savoie with Red Currant Jam

Serves 4

1 tablespoon hulled unsalted pumpkin
   seeds
5¼ ounces (150 g) red currant jam
1 teaspoon mustard seeds
Pinch of Espelette pepper
1 Tomme de Savoie cheese (semi-firm
   cow's-milk cheese)
Pain d'épice (French spice bread;
   see Note page 28), sliced and toasted

Skillet

Preparation time: 5 minutes

Cooking time: about 3 minutes

Toast the pumpkin seeds for a few minutes in a dry skillet.

In a small bowl, mix together the pumpkin seeds, jam, mustard seeds, and pepper.

Serve the cheese with the jam and pain d'épice.

Roquefort with Butter and Celery

Serves 4

½ stalk celery
4 fresh chives
1 bunch radishes
7 ounces (200 g) Roquefort cheese
7 tablespoons (100 g) salted butter, at room
    temperature
Brioche, for serving

🕐 Preparation time: 5 minutes

Finely chop the celery and chives. Cut 2 radishes into thin matchsticks.

In a small bowl, mix together the celery, chives, cheese, butter, and radish matchsticks using a fork.

Serve with brioche and the rest of the radishes.

Drinks Time

5 different cheeses

For serving with wine or
cocktails, with fresh herbs,
vegetables for nibbling,
butter for spreading, jam . . .

ripened goat cheese
Morbier
Camembert
Saint-Nectaire
sheep's-milk Tomme

Desk Time

5 hard cheeses

Easy to eat without making a
mess—your computer will
thank you. Serve with
dried fruit, crackers . . .

Cantal
Comté
aged Mimolette
goat's-milk Tomme
Tomme de Savoie

Bedtime

5 soft cheeses, soft as a pillow

For a midnight snack, serve
with pain d'épice (see Note
page 28), brioche, and honey.

fresh goat cheese
young Brie
fromage blanc
Reblochon
Saint-Félicien

Friends' Time

5 strong cheeses

For bad breath between buddies, serve with spices to liven things up.

Fourme de Montbrison
Bleu d'Auvergne
aged goat cheese
Munster
mystery cheese, for blind tasting

Desserts

Strawberries, Apples, and Almonds

Serves 4

2 Granny Smith apples
1 pound (500 g) ripe strawberries
2 lemons
½ cup (50 g) sliced almonds
1 tablespoon honey
1 bunch fresh mint

Baking dish

360°F (180°C) oven

Preparation time: 10 minutes

Cooking time: 15 minutes

Preheat the oven to 360°F (180°C).

Peel and core the apples and cut them into pieces. Hull the strawberries. Zest one of the lemons and juice both.

In a small bowl, stir together the lemon juice and honey.

Arrange the fruit in a baking dish, add the almonds, lemon zest, and mint leaves, and drizzle with the lemon juice mixture.

Cover with aluminum foil and bake for 15 minutes, until the fruit is warm.

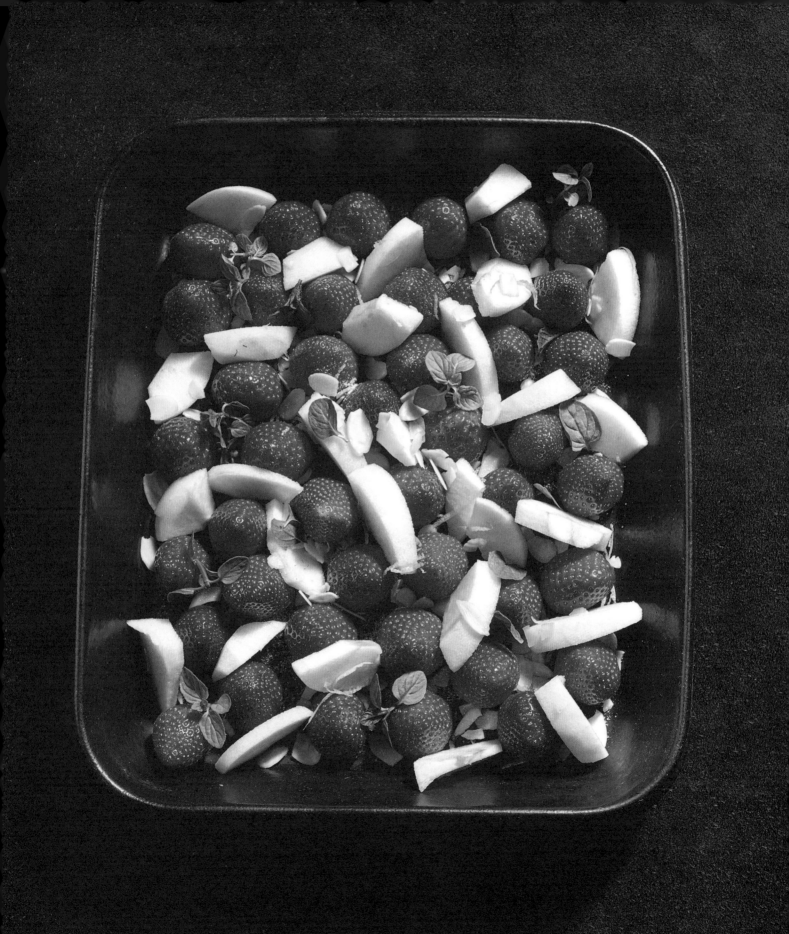

Apples with Cherry Jam and Calvados

Serves 4

4 apples, such as Pink Lady
3½ ounces (100 g) black cherry jam
⅔ cup (150 ml) Calvados
6 tablespoons (¾ stick/80 g) butter
3 tablespoons superfine sugar

Apple corer
Baking dish

360°F (180°C) oven

Preparation time: 10 minutes

Cooking time: 30 minutes

Preheat the oven to 360°F (180°C).

Cut a lid from the tops of the apples and remove the cores with an apple corer.

Put the apples in a baking dish. In a small bowl, mix the jam with the Calvados. Cut the butter into six pieces.

Fill the apples with the jam and place the lids back on top. Place a small knob of the butter on each apple, sprinkle evenly with the sugar, and bake for 30 minutes, until the apples are tender.

Spoon over the juice from the baking dish before serving.

Poached Pears

Serves 4

4 firm pears
2 vanilla beans
2 unwaxed oranges
2 ounces (50 g) fresh ginger
1¼ cups (250 g) sugar
3 cinnamon sticks

Dutch oven

Preparation time: 10 minutes

Cooking time: 30-40 minutes

Peel the pears. Halve the vanilla beans lengthwise. Cut the oranges into pieces without peeling them. Peel and slice the ginger.

In a Dutch oven, combine 4½ cups (1 L) water, the orange wedges, ginger, sugar, cinnamon, and vanilla bean pod and seeds. Bring to a boil.

Place the whole pears in the syrup and cook over medium-low heat for 30 to 40 minutes, depending on the firmness of the pears, until they are tender when pierced with a sharp knife, and then serve.

Apples with Salted Butter

Serves 4

6 apples, such as Pink Lady
10 tablespoons (1¼ sticks/150 g)
    salted butter
½ cup (100 g) superfine sugar

Apple corer
Mandoline
Dutch oven

320°F (160°C) oven

Preparation time: 15 minutes

Cooking time: 1 hour 5 minutes

Preheat the oven to 320°F (160°C).

Peel the apples and core them with an apple corer. Slice them into thin rings using a mandoline. Thinly slice the butter.

Sprinkle some of the sugar over the bottom of a round Dutch oven and top with a few slices of the butter. Arrange a layer of apple slices on top in a rosette pattern. Top with more butter and sugar and another layer of apples. Repeat this layering until you have used all the apples. Cover and bake for 30 minutes.

Remove the lid of the Dutch oven and bake for 30 minutes more, until the sugar is caramelized.

Let cool completely. To unmold, place the cooled Dutch oven in a very hot oven for 5 minutes, then immediately turn over the apples onto a serving plate, before serving.

Pineapple with Hazelnuts and Vanilla

Serves 4

1 good-looking pineapple
1 vanilla bean
7 tablespoons (80 g) sugar
6 tablespoons (¾ stick/80 g) butter
⅔ cup (150 ml) rum
Generous ⅓ cup (50 g) hazelnuts

Saucepan
Dutch oven

300°F (150°C) oven

Preparation time: 10 minutes

Cooking time: 50 minutes

Preheat the oven to 300°F (150°C).

Peel the pineapple, taking care to remove the eyes. Halve the vanilla bean lengthwise and scrape out the seeds.

In a small saucepan, heat the sugar over medium-high heat, without stirring, until the sugar melts into caramel, about 10 minutes. If necessary, brush down any crystals that form on the side of the pot with a damp pastry brush.

Add the butter, rum, and vanilla bean pod and seeds. Stir to melt the butter and combine.

Place the pineapple in the Dutch oven, cover with the rum-flavored caramel, and add the hazelnuts.

Bake for 40 minutes, basting the pineapple with the caramel frequently during cooking, until it is tender, and then serve immediately.

Apricot Gratin

Serves 4

9 tablespoons (125 g) butter
12 ripe apricots
⅔ cup (125 g) superfine sugar
1 cup (125 g) almond meal
2 eggs

Baking dish

360°F (180°C) oven
Resting time: 1 hour

Preparation time: 15 minutes

Cooking time: 20 minutes

Take the butter out of the refrigerator at least 1 hour before starting the dish so it is very soft. Preheat the oven to 360°F (180°C).

Halve and pit the apricots. In a medium bowl, mash the soft butter with a spatula until creamy. Mix in the sugar and almond meal, then add the eggs.

Pour the almond mixture into a baking dish, arrange the apricots cut side up on top.

Bake for 20 minutes, until the gratin is browned, and then serve.

Pink Praline Semolina Cake

Serves 4

4½ cups (1 L) milk
6 ounces (170 g) candied almonds
   (see Note), crushed
9 tablespoons (100 g) fine semolina

Dutch oven

Preparation time: 5 minutes

Cooking time: 10 minutes
Resting time: 1 hour

In a Dutch oven, combine the milk and 5¼ ounces (150 g) of the crushed almonds. Bring to a boil, then cook for 5 minutes to melt the praline. While stirring continuously, add the semolina in a steady stream and cook for 5 minutes more.

Let the mixture cool for 1 hour, then transfer to the refrigerator to cool completely.

Scatter the remaining crushed almonds over the top before serving.

Note: In Lyon, candied almonds are colored pink. Use them if you can find them, or add a few drops of food coloring if you'd like.

Ultimate Crumble

Serves 4

10½ ounces (300 g) fresh or frozen berries
7 tablespoons (100 g) salted butter
½ cup (100 g) sugar
¾ cup (100 g) all-purpose flour
7 tablespoons (50 g) almond meal
½ cup (50 g) hazelnut meal

Baking dish

360°F (180°C) oven

Preparation time: 10 minutes

Cooking time: 30 minutes

Preheat the oven to 360°F (180°C).

Arrange the berries in a baking dish. Cut the butter into cubes.

In a medium bowl, mix together the butter, sugar, flour, almond meal, and hazelnut meal with a fork. Finish mixing with your fingers to make a crumbly mixture.

Cover the fruit with the crumb topping and bake for 30 minutes, until the fruit is bubbly. Serve immediately.

Pineapple Clafoutis

Serves 4

1½ (8-ounce/340-g) cans pineapple rings
   in juice
3 eggs
14 tablespoons (175 g) superfine sugar
¾ cup (100 g) all-purpose flour
¼ teaspoon baking powder
1 cup (250 ml) milk
3 tablespoons (40 g) butter, melted

Baking dish

360°F (180°C) oven

Preparation time: 5 minutes

Cooking time: 40 minutes

Preheat the oven to 360°F (180°C).

Drain the pineapple slices in a strainer.

In a medium bowl, whisk the eggs and 10 tablespoons (125 g) of the sugar until the mixture is pale and creamy. Add the flour, baking powder, milk, and melted butter.

Pour the mixture into a baking dish, arrange the pineapple rings on top, and bake for 35 minutes, until the cake is golden brown.

Sprinkle with the remaining 4 tablespoons (50 g) sugar and bake for 5 minutes more, before serving.

Ultimate Apple Tart

Serves 4

6 Pink Lady apples
6 tablespoons (¾ stick/80 g) butter
1 large disk or sheet frozen puff pastry,
  thawed
½ cup plus 1 tablespoon (100 g) sugar
⅓ cup (60 g) medium-grind semolina

Apple corer
Baking dish

360°F (180°C) oven

Preparation time: 20 minutes

Cooking time: 45 minutes
Resting time: 20 minutes

Preheat the oven to 360°F (180°C).

Peel the apples and core them with an apple corer. Slice them into thin rings. Cut the butter into small pieces.

Lay out the puff pastry on a baking sheet, keeping the parchment paper backing underneath. Lift the pastry up and sprinkle half of the sugar underneath. Sprinkle the semolina on top of the pastry, then arrange the apple slices over the semolina in a rosette pattern. Dot the top with the butter and sprinkle evenly with the remaining half of sugar. Bake for 45 minutes. The apples should be golden brown and the pastry crisp.

Let cool before serving: The caramel that forms on the underside of the pastry needs to set to unstick.

Bread Pudding

Serves 4

14 ounces (400 g) brioche or challah
7 ounces (200 g) pain d'épice (French
    spice bread; see Note, page 28)
4 eggs
⅔ cup (125 g) sugar
6 tablespoons (100 ml) rum
2 cups (500 ml) milk
⅓ cup (50 g) raisins

- Dutch oven
- 360°F (180°C) oven
- Preparation time: 10 minutes
- Cooking time: 40 minutes

Preheat the oven to 360°F (180°C).

Cut the brioche and pain d'épice into cubes.

In a large bowl, whisk the eggs with the sugar. Add the rum and milk and whisk to combine. Add the cubes of brioche and pain d'épice, making sure they are well soaked, then fold in the raisins.

Pour the mixture into a Dutch oven.

Bake for 40 minutes, until the top is golden brown, and then serve.

Brioche Perdue

Serves 4

6 tablespoons (¾ stick/80 g) butter
3 eggs
1¼ cups (300 ml) heavy cream
1 tablespoon honey
8 slices brioche or challah
2 tablespoons superfine sugar

Large baking dish

Broiler

Preparation time: 5 minutes

Cooking time: 7 minutes

Preheat the broiler.

Put the butter in a large baking dish and place it under the broiler for 2 minutes to melt.

In a shallow bowl, beat the eggs with the cream and honey until combined. Soak the brioche slices in the egg mixture on both sides. Carefully lay the brioche slices in the dish in a single layer over the melted butter, sprinkle with the sugar.

Broil for 5 minutes, until the tops are golden brown. Serve immediately.

Rice Pudding

Serves 4

1 organic unwaxed orange, scrubbed
1 vanilla bean
4½ cups (1 L) whole milk
½ cup (100 g) superfine sugar
½ cup (100 g) short-grain rice

Dutch oven

Preparation time: 5 minutes

Cooking time: 45 minutes

Small dice the orange without peeling it. Split the vanilla bean in half lengthwise and scrape out the seeds.

In a Dutch oven, combine the milk, sugar, orange cubes, and vanilla bean pod and seeds. Bring to a boil. Pour in the rice in a stream, stirring continuously. Cook, stirring, over low heat for 45 minutes, until the milk is absorbed and the rice is tender.

Let cool to room temperature and remove and discard the vanilla bean pod before serving.

Mixed Fruit Compote

Serves 4

2 apples
6 ripe apricots
3½ ounces (100 g) sweet cherries
2 ripe nectarines
1 ounce (30 g) fresh ginger
⅔ cup (150 ml) sparkling lemonade, such as
   Lorina or San Pellegrino

Dutch oven
Food processor

Preparation time: 10 minutes

Cooking time: 15 minutes

Peel, slice, and core the apples. Halve and pit the apricots, cherries, and nectarines. Peel the ginger and slice into matchsticks.

In a Dutch oven, combine the fruit, ginger, and lemonade and simmer over medium-low heat, covered, for 15 minutes.

Puree in a food processor, until the fruit is combined but still chunky, and then serve.

Muscat Peaches with Verbena

Serves 4

4 beautiful ripe peaches
¾ cup (200 ml) Muscat de Rivesaltes or
   other fortified wine
¼ cup (½ stick/50 g) butter
1½ tablespoons brown sugar
2 sprigs fresh lemon verbena

Dutch oven

Preparation time: 10 minutes

Cooking time: 10 minutes

Bring a Dutch oven filled with water to a boil. Add the peaches and blanch for 1 minute, then remove them with a slotted spoon and run them under cold water.

Drain and dry the Dutch oven. Peel the peaches and arrange the whole fruits in the pot, add the Muscat, butter, brown sugar, and lemon verbena sprigs.

Cover and cook over medium-low heat for 10 minutes, until the peaches are tender.

Let cool until just warm before serving with some of the sauce.

Prunes in Spiced Wine

Serves 4

3 cups (400 g) pitted prunes
2 cups (500 ml) good red wine
6 tablespoons (100 ml) kirsch
1 teaspoon ground cinnamon
Pinch of grated nutmeg
2 ounces (50 g) fresh ginger
3 star anise pods
Zest of 1 lemon
½ cup plus 1½ tablespoons (120 g) packed
   brown sugar

Dutch oven

Preparation time: 5 minutes

Cooking time: 1 hour 5 minutes

Put all the ingredients in a Dutch oven. Bring to a boil, cover, and cook over low heat for 1 hour, until the prunes are very soft.

Let cool before serving. Keeps for 1 month in the refrigerator.

INDEX OF RECIPES

INDEX OF INGREDIENTS

Editor: Laura Dozier
Cover design and typesetting: Darilyn Lowe Carnes
Production Manager: Kathleen Gaffney

Library of Congress Control Number: 2017930295

ISBN: 978-1-4197-2746-7

Originally published in French under the title *Un couteau, Un plat, Une cocotte* by Hachette Livre (Marabout) 2016

Printed and bound in China
10 9 8 7 6 5 4 3 2 1

Abrams books are available at special discounts when purchased in quantity for premiums and promotions as well as fundraising or educational use. Special editions can also be created to specification. For details, contact specialsales@abramsbooks.com or the address below.

ABRAMS The Art of Books
115 West 18th Street, New York, NY 10011
abramsbooks.com